ROUTLEDGE LIBRARY EDITIONS: LIBRARY AND INFORMATION SCIENCE

Volume 88

SCI-TECH LIBRARIES SERVING ZOOLOGICAL GARDENS

SCI-TECH LIBRARIES SERVING ZOOLOGICAL GARDENS

Edited by
ELLIS MOUNT

LONDON AND NEW YORK

First published in 1988 by The Haworth Press, Inc.

This edition first published in 2020
by Routledge
2 Park Square, Milton Park, Abingdon, Oxon OX14 4RN

and by Routledge
52 Vanderbilt Avenue, New York, NY 10017

Routledge is an imprint of the Taylor & Francis Group, an informa business

© 1988 The Haworth Press, Inc.

All rights reserved. No part of this book may be reprinted or reproduced or utilised in any form or by any electronic, mechanical, or other means, now known or hereafter invented, including photocopying and recording, or in any information storage or retrieval system, without permission in writing from the publishers.

Trademark notice: Product or corporate names may be trademarks or registered trademarks, and are used only for identification and explanation without intent to infringe.

British Library Cataloguing in Publication Data
A catalogue record for this book is available from the British Library

ISBN: 978-0-367-34616-4 (Set)
ISBN: 978-0-429-34352-0 (Set) (ebk)
ISBN: 978-0-367-36369-7 (Volume 88) (hbk)
ISBN: 978-0-367-36373-4 (Volume 88) (pbk)
ISBN: 978-0-429-34550-0 (Volume 88) (ebk)

Publisher's Note
The publisher has gone to great lengths to ensure the quality of this reprint but points out that some imperfections in the original copies may be apparent.

Disclaimer
The publisher has made every effort to trace copyright holders and would welcome correspondence from those they have been unable to trace.

Sci-Tech Libraries Serving Zoological Gardens

Ellis Mount
Editor

The Haworth Press
New York • London

Sci-Tech Libraries Serving Zoological Gardens has also been published as *Science & Technology Libraries*, Volume 8, Number 4 1988.

© 1988 by The Haworth Press, Inc. All rights reserved. No part of this work may be reproduced or utilized in any form or by any means, electronic or mechanical, including photocopying, microfilm, and recording, or by any other information storage and retrieval system, without permission in writing from the publisher. Printed in the United States of America.

The Haworth Press, Inc., 12 West 32 Street, New York, NY 10001
EUROSPAN/Haworth, 3 Henrietta Street, London WC2E 8LU England

LIBRARY OF CONGRESS
Library of Congress Cataloging-in-Publication Data

Sci-Tech libraries serving zoological gardens / Ellis Mount, editor.
    p. cm.
    "Has also been published as Science & technology libraries, volume 8, number 4, 1988" — T.p. verso.
    Includes bibliographical references.
ISBN 0-86656-837-9
1. Zoological libraries—United States. 2. Zoos—Bibliography—Methodology. 3. Zoo animals—Bibliography—Methodology. I. Mount, Ellis.
Z675.Z66S35 1988   88-17548
026.591--dc19   CIP

Sci-Tech Libraries
Serving Zoological Gardens

CONTENTS

Introduction *Ellis Mount*	xiii
National Zoological Park Branch Library *Kay A. Kenyon*	1
Introduction	1
History	2
Collection	2
Programs of NZP	4
Services	5
Networking	6
Future Plans	7
Lincoln Park Zoological Gardens Reference Library *Joyce M. Shaw*	9
Introduction	9
History of Lincoln Park Zoo	10
History of the Library	11
Scientific Collections	12
Special Collections	12
Services	13
IMS Conservation Project	14
Zoo 2000	15
New York Zoological Society Library *Steven P. Johnson*	21
Institutional Setting	21
Collections	23
History of the Collection and Facilities	24
Special Collections	26
Staffing and Organizational Setting	27
Computer Applications	28
Relationships with Other Libraries	28

Zoological Society of San Diego Library 33
Michaele M. Robinson

Zoological Society of San Diego 33
Ernst Schwarz 34
Main Library and Satellites 35
Services, Staff, Operations 35

Minnesota Zoological Garden Library 39
Angela Norell

History and Description 39
Collection 40
Services 41
Users 42

Cincinnati Zoo Library 45
Beatrice Orendorff

Facilities and Collections 45
Services 46

American Zoological Park Libraries and Archives: Historical Considerations and Their Current Status 49
Vernon N. Kisling, Jr.

An Historical Perspective 49
Contemporary Collections, Management, and Services 50
The Archive Collections 58

SCI-TECH COLLECTIONS 61
Tony Stankus, Editor

Superconductivity: A Brief Guide to the Research and Literature 63
C. Herbert Carson
James A. Barrett
Mary Jean Colburn

Introduction 63
Current and Potential Applications 66
Monographs 68
Indices and Databases 69

    Nonprint Resources   71
    Conclusions   72

**NEW REFERENCE WORKS IN SCIENCE
    AND TECHNOLOGY**   77
        Robert G. Krupp, Editor

SCI-TECH ONLINE   99
        Ellen Nagle, Editor

SCI-TECH IN REVIEW   107
        Karla J. Pearce, Editor
        Giuliana Lavendel, Associate Editor

Introduction

Most people visiting a zoo probably give no thought to the existence of special libraries serving zoo employees. As a matter of fact, most special librarians visiting a zoo probably don't realize that the zoo might very well be served by a library or information center. The fact that zoo libraries are so little known has prompted the selection of such libraries as the theme for an issue.

This issue contains descriptions of the libraries serving six American zoos, ranging from some of the largest and oldest to those which are smaller and younger. The type of collections and their services might be surprising to those who are not familiar with such libraries. In addition the issue includes a survey made of zoo libraries.

The first paper, by Kay A. Kenyon, describes the library at the National Zoological Park in Washington, D.C., a branch of the Smithsonian Institution Libraries. Next is the paper describing the library at the Lincoln Park Zoo in Chicago, written by Joyce M. Shaw.

The library of the New York Zoological Society is discussed by Steven P. Johnson. Next is the paper by Michaele M. Robinson on the zoo library in San Diego.

The Minnesota Zoological Garden Library in St. Paul is described by Angela Norell's paper. This is followed by a description of the Cincinnati Zoo Library, written by Beatrice Orendorff.

A special survey of American zoo libraries follows next, prepared by Vernon N. Kisling, Jr. He presents data on 78 libraries in regard to their staffing, facilities, collections and services, as well as data on 32 archive collections.

The special collections paper for this issue deals with a very timely subject, namely superconductors. It was prepared by C. Herbert Carson, James A. Barrett and Mary Jean Colburn.

Our regular features complete the issue.

Ellis Mount
Editor

© 1988 by The Haworth Press, Inc. All rights reserved.

National Zoological Park Branch Library

Kay A. Kenyon

SUMMARY. The National Zoological Park Branch of the Smithsonian Institution Libraries is dedicated to supporting the specialized information needs of the Zoo in its commitment to science, education, recreation, and conservation. The library's history, collection, programs, services, and relations with other zoo libraries are described.

INTRODUCTION

The National Zoological Park (NZP) Branch library is one of an increasing number of zoo and aquarium libraries which have been created or expanded to support their institutions' goals in the areas of education, research, recreation, and conservation.

Unlike other zoo libraries, the NZP Branch is part of a larger library system—the Smithsonian Institution Libraries (SIL). While only one professional librarian provides on-site services such as reference, circulation, interlibrary loans, and collection development and management, a centrally located team of other SIL staff provides support services such as administration, acquisitions, cataloging, and book conservation.

The purpose of the NZP Branch of the SIL is to supply the information and research needs of the staff at the National Zoo, e.g., curators, keepers, researchers, veterinarians, pathologists, lab technicians, nutritionists, educators, administrators. There are 320 permanent Zoo staff members plus numerous part-time and visiting

---

Kay A. Kenyon is Chief Librarian at the National Zoological Park Branch Smithsonian Institution Libraries, Washington, D.C. 20008. She has the following degrees: MA in Library Science, University of Denver, BA in English, Cedar Crest College, Allentown, PA.

© 1988 by The Haworth Press, Inc. All rights reserved.

researchers. The zoo library staff also responds to inquiries from other Smithsonian staff, scholars, scientists, writers, and the general public in the fields of zoology, veterinary medicine, and related disciplines. It also serves as a major link in the national network of zoo and aquarium libraries by supporting a newsletter, preparing bibliographies, and participating in other cooperative activities.

HISTORY

The history of the NZP Branch parallels the history of the National Zoological Park. Established in 1898, the year of the Zoo's founding, the library, housed in the administrative building (Holt House), began as a small collection of books and pamphlets on animal management and zoology. Over the next few decades, the library grew slowly. SIL provided some assistance, especially in cataloging and binding. Then, in the late 1960s and early 1970s, the Zoo expanded, adding new departments, exhibits, programs, and staff. In turn, the library grew to accommodate the needs generated by the Zoo's rapid growth. In 1972 SIL sent a professional librarian to the Zoo part-time to manage the collection. In 1973 the library was relocated to the Hospital/Research building. Four years later, after outgrowing that space, it was moved to its present location in the Education/Administration Building. In 1975 the Zoo acquired a 3,150-acre conservation and research facility near Front Royal, Virginia. A collection of materials was established on-site under the direction of the Zoo librarian. In 1979 the first full-time professional librarian was hired. Since that time, the library has steadily increased its holdings and added selected subjects such as horticulture and invertebrates, reflecting the Zoo's goal of integrating plants and animals into a biological park concept.

COLLECTION

The NZP Branch's collection consists of approximately 3,700 monographs, 3,300 bound journal volumes (320 current periodical titles), and over 9,000 unbound pieces and ephemera. The library currently collects material in the fields of animal behavior, care of captive animals, veterinary medicine, pathology, animal nutrition, ecology, animal conservation and endangered species, zoology, and horticulture. Like most zoo libraries, the NZP Branch maintains a collection of zoo and aquarium ephemera including newsletters, annual reports, animal inventories, brochures, and studbooks. It also keeps NZP's annual reports and the publications of its staff. Most of the Zoo's archival material, however, is housed in the Smithsonian Archives.

The collection emphasizes current material. However, there is a small collection of old books and journals dating from the mid-1800s. Any rare book found in the collection is transferred to SIL's Special Collections Branch, which has a temperature and humidity controlled atmosphere.

The collection is primarily in English, with some German material, and is composed mainly of American and European imprints plus a few serials published in Africa, Japan, and Australia.

Although the librarian generally uses the indexes found in online databases, the library does own the printed version of *Zoological Record* (Sections *Pisces, Mammalia, Aves, and Reptilia and Amphibia*) dating back to volume 1 (1864). It also acquires frequently-used abstracting tools such as *Veterinary Bulletin, Animal Behavior Abstracts, Nutrition Abstracts Series A & B,* and *Wildlife Disease Review*.

Most of the serial subscriptions in the collection are technical and specialized, such as *Journal of Zoo Animal Medicine* and *Zoo Biology*, although there are a few serial subscriptions to general magazines such as *Audubon* and *National Wildlife*. Other valuable resources found in the collection include older titles such as the *Proceedings of the Zoological Society of London* dating from volume 1 (1832), and *Journal of Mammalogy* dating from volume 1 (1919-1920). The library also owns a complete set of the *Proceedings of the International Symposium on Diseases in Zoo Animals*.

In maintaining the collection, the NZP Branch is fortunate to have its valuable books repaired by the SIL's Book Conservation Laboratory. New items, paperbound monographs and serials, and routine repairs, are sent to a commercial bindery through the SIL Binding Unit.

Access to the collection is through two computer terminals in the branch and others located throughout the SIL system. NZP Branch holdings are included with the other SIL holdings in an online catalog, i.e., the Smithsonian Institution Bibliographic Information System (SIBIS). Manufactured by Geac and modified for SIL, access is by author, title, author-title, subject, keyword, and number (call number, ISBN, OCLC). Being "user-friendly," SIBIS has been greeted with much enthusiasm by zoo staff. The librarian also uses two other modules on SIBIS—Acquisitions and E-mail. Two others, Serial Records and Circulation, are in the planning stages.

PROGRAMS OF NZP

The library's function is to supply the information needs of the NZP staff. This section describes some of the long-term goals and programs of the National Zoo as they affect the NZP Branch library's operation.

The National Zoological Park is dedicated to

> public education about the welfare of animals, recreation of visitors, advancement of biological and veterinary science, and conservation. In cooperation with zoos throughout the world, the National Zoo works to save endangered species by using the most modern techniques of reproductive biology and animal husbandry and by promoting habitat preservation.[1]

The animal departments (made up of curators and keepers) focus on the care, exhibition, and study of the animals in the zoo from the largest African elephant to the smallest hissing cockroach. The Zoo is increasing its focus on invertebrates and on plant/animal mixed species enclosures that create a more natural ecosystem. The animal departments also contribute to education and aid other zoos. The Departments of Animal Health and of Pathology investigate the causes, prevention, and treatment of disease in captive animals. They examine problems of reproductive physiology. The medical departments also play a major role in pre- and post-doctoral training of zoo veterinarians and other medical specialists. The Department of Zoological Research provides scientific support for conservation, research, and education. It also promotes cooperative exploration of general research problems with scientists from other institutions. The research staff studies animal communication, genetics, reintroduction of animals into the wild, and nutritional studies of mammal milk composition. The Department of Conservation is dedicated to saving rare and endangered species by breeding programs and research. It aims to further the cause of tropical conservation, particularly by offering a wildlife conservation training course to students from developing nations. The library also supports zoo field researchers working in countries such as Brazil, Sri Lanka, and Venezuela.

The NZP Branch provides services and materials to other departments as well. The Office of Education supplies information to visitors about such issues as the role of zoos in wildlife conservation and develops learning labs, school and outreach programs, and exhibits. The Office of Public Affairs organizes public lectures, symposiums, news releases and other public events. The Registrar tracks animal regulations, animal transport, and animal records. The Office of Management Services is involved in personnel and accounting. The library also serves support services such as the Office of Facilities Management, the Office of Police and Safety, and the Office of Design and Exhibit Planning. Within the support units the library especially supports the Horticulturist and Landscaping units. The library also provides services to the permanent staff of FONZ (Friends of the National Zoo), although its docents and volunteers rely primarily on FONZ's own small collection of books.

SERVICES

A zoo library's location poses a special challenge because staff in a zoo are spread out throughout the institution. At the National Zoo, the library shares a building with the administrative and education offices and FONZ at one end of the Zoo's 163-acre park. The hospital and research staffs are located at the opposite end of the park. The animal curators, keepers, and support staff are distributed in the middle. The staff at the Conservation and Research Center in Front Royal is sixty miles away.

The National Zoological Park Branch has met this challenge by bringing the library to the staff. Some reference material is duplicated and about half of the library's book collection is distributed in various locations throughout the park on indefinite loan. These subcollections are maintained by the librarian. The librarian also routes a monthly "current awareness bulletin" to staff at NZP as well as to the Conservation Center and to affiliated researchers working in Brazil and Venezuela. This bulletin includes the tables of contents of current journals and a list of new acquisitions.

The Branch library also provides the staff with online literature searches using DIALOG. The most often used databases include BIOSIS, CAB ABSTRACTS, LIFE SCIENCES, ZOOLOGICAL RECORD, and MEDLINE. Searches may include any topic from the captive management of beavers or calcium balance of lizards to artificial insemination of pandas or pathology of the golden lion tamarin. The librarian also produces bibliographies upon request. A microcomputer with its word processing capabilities has proven helpful in this endeavor.

The NZP Branch also borrows from other libraries. It relies heavily on loans from other SIL branches such as the National Museum of Natural History and Office of Horticulture Branches, and from other area libraries such as the National Agricultural Library, the National Library of Medicine, and the Library of Congress. Access to the OCLC database, as well as the use of a commercial document delivery service, helps in locating and obtaining materials.

The public may use the zoo library by appointment during working hours, 8:00 am-4:30 pm, Monday through Friday. Reference service is available, but material must be used on the premises. Photocopying is available for a charge. The public may also borrow materials through their local libraries on interlibrary loan.

NETWORKING

The NZP Branch library serves as a major link between other zoo and aquarium librarians. Most zoo and aquarium librarians are members of the American Association of Zoological Park and Aquarium Librarians Special Interest Group (AAZPA/LSIG). The LSIG meet once a year at the AAZPA Annual Conferences. Its newsletter, *Library News for Zoos and Aquariums*,[2] is edited and produced three times a year at the National Zoo library. Circulating to more than 200 zoo people, it serves a dual purpose — it is a forum for communication and sharing of materials and ideas among zoo and aquarium librarians, and it is an important communication link between zoo and aquarium librarians and zoo professional staff. Members of the LSIG as well as the NZP Branch Librarian produce and share bibliographies for the zoo profession and often provide library services to those zoos without librarians. More and more zoo librarians are being asked to advise zoos anticipating expansion or creation of libraries at their institutions. The NZP librarian is also a member of the Special Libraries Association (SLA) and occasionally receives information and advice from this organization.

FUTURE PLANS

The National Zoological Park Branch library expects a slowing down of new acquisitions due to limited space and escalating serial prices. However, with the help of SIL, it will continue to provide professional library service to the Zoo. Cooperation with other zoo librarians will continue to increase as the need for libraries in zoos grows.

FIGURE 1

STATISTICS

Name of Zoo	National Zoological Park Washington, D.C.
Date Founded	1898
Name of Library	National Zoological Park Branch, Smithsonian Institution Libraries
Telephone	202/673-4771
Name of Library Director	Kay A. Kenyon, Chief Librarian
Library Collection Size	
Number of Monographs	3,700
Number of Bound Journals	3,300
Number of Subscriptions	300
Main Subjects Collected	Animal behavior, veterinary medicine, pathology, animal nutrition, zoology, wildlife conservation and endangered species, ecology, horticulture
Staff size	1 Professional
Online searching done	Yes (for SI staff only)
Interlibrary loans made	Yes
Names of network affiliations	OCLC, American Association of Zoological Parks and Aquariums Librarians Special Interest Group

NOTES

1. *Smithsonian Year 1986*. Washington, D.C.: Smithsonian Institution Press, 1987: p. 63.

2. *Library News for Zoos and Aquariums*. Oct 1982— . Published tri-yearly by Smithsonian Institution Libraries, National Zoological Park Branch, Washington, D.C. 20008, Kay Kenyon, ed.

Lincoln Park Zoological Gardens Reference Library

Joyce M. Shaw

SUMMARY. Lincoln Park Zoological Gardens, founded in 1868, is supported in its goals and purposes by its reference library. The library offers a full range of services based on its specialized reference collections. In addition to a description of these features, the paper contains an introduction to zoos as societal entities, and the future trends in information requirements of zoos are discussed. An appendix provides a bibliography of articles on libraries and information services in zoos and aquariums.

INTRODUCTION

Man's complex relationship with wild animals dates from prehistoric times. Animals have been revered, feared and tamed. The history of zoological gardens may be traced alongside the time scale charting the movement of human civilization. As kingdoms rose in Asia and the Middle East, man continued to define and dominate his involvement with wild animals by creating private menageries to entertain and honor royal rulers. These zoological gardens of old displayed animals as trophies and oddities. Over the centuries cities and governments laid claim to the regal privilege of owning and displaying wildlife. By the beginning of the 19th century, major

---

Joyce M. Shaw is Zoo Librarian, Lincoln Park Zoological Gardens Reference Library, 2200 North Cannon Drive, Chicago, IL 60614-3895. She has a BA degree from the University of New Orleans and an MA degree from Roosevelt University in Chicago.

The author thanks P. Piasecki for her review of the first draft, J. Tuohy for editorial comments, W. Schmidt for research assistance, and G. Callis for word processing support. Lincoln Park Zoological Society is thanked for funding the library.

© 1988 by The Haworth Press, Inc. All rights reserved.

cities in Europe (Vienna, London, Paris, and Berlin) hosted wild beasts within their borders. In the United States, zoological gardens were established as public entities in Chicago, Philadelphia, New York City, and Washington, D.C. by the late 1800s.[1]

The early philosophy of animal display, man's dominance over beast and curiosity for the unusual, has significantly changed over the centuries. When the Zoological Society of London stated a dual purpose in 1826 — to introduce new animals from foreign lands *and* to advance the science of zoology — the new role of the zoological garden in society was undeniably developing as conservator and protector of animal life.

Modern zoological gardens, both here and abroad, have assigned themselves the difficult task of saving the world. If not the responsibility of saving the world as a whole, then the enormous burden of preserving the tiny parts of life comprising the varied animals species inhabiting this planet. This complex philosophical purpose based on a responsible commitment to captive wildlife illustrates the evolution in thought concerning man's relationship with wild animals. As a result, the national organization charged with monitoring and accrediting zoological gardens and aquariums (American Association of Zoological Parks and Aquariums), succinctly articulated the goals of the modern zoo as "recreation, conservation, education and research."[2]

HISTORY OF LINCOLN PARK ZOO

> The Board was made the recipients during the year of an agreeable expression of courtesy and good will from the Commissioners of Central Park, New York, by the donation, through O. B. Green, Esq., of a pair of swans, taken from Central Park. They were placed at Lincoln Park, affording much pleasure to the visitors.[3]

Lincoln Park Zoo, founded in 1868, is one of the oldest zoological gardens in North America. As other donations were placed alongside the swans which began the animal collection in the park, the small menagerie located on eleven acres of Chicago's lakefront, grew steadily during its early years. In 1874, an inventory of the park's animal residents included 13 swans, two buffalo, three wolves — 71 birds and mammals in all. During the zoo's first quarter century, the decision was made that "whatever the animal collection in Lincoln Park might be, it should always be free to the public."[4] One hundred twenty years later, one of the last free zoos in America proudly hosts an animal collection of world-class significance and is an acknowledged leader in education, conservation and research among zoos. It is owned and operated by the Chicago Park District and receives additional funding from the Lincoln Park Zoological Society.

HISTORY OF THE LIBRARY

Libraries, as a functional component in zoological gardens, are a phenomenon of modern times. A few existed before the turn of the century, but the majority were started within the last twenty years with eighty percent of those opening less than seven years ago.[5] Lincoln Park Zoo Library opened its doors to the public in December 1980.

Lincoln Park Zoo Library owes its creation to three things: the information demands of zoo personnel, the interest of Lincoln Park Zoological Society's Women's Board and the cooperative spirit of zoo administrators and volunteers. In 1978, Mrs. Julian Harvey, a Women's Board member and former librarian, recognized the need for coordinating information services at the zoo and joined with zoo staff to become a driving force in establishing and organizing the library. She enlisted Walter L. Necker, a retired bio-medical librarian from the University of Chicago and long-time naturalist, as volunteer library consultant. Under his experienced guidance, paid and volunteer helpers sorted and organized crates and boxes of books, journals and reprints. Space for the new library was allocated in the former office of the zoo, two rooms in the Primate House. After nine months of work, Mr. Necker submitted his progress report to the zoo's administration " . . . it is a collection superior to that in the average American Zoo."[6] Mr. Necker outlined in his report his scheme for classification of materials and his ideas for special collections to be owned by the library. However, he was not able to see his plans fulfilled. His death in December 1979 left his work in the hands of volunteers until 1980 when a professional librarian was hired. The "Walter Necker Reading Room" was later designated in recognition of his contribution to the library.

With continuing support from the Lincoln Park Zoological Society, the library has built a collection of basic and specialized zoological research materials and is a unique informational resource in the community.

SCIENTIFIC COLLECTIONS

The library's scientific collection consists of approximately 2,000 books in zoology (emphasizing animals in the collection), veterinary medicine, conservation biology, and zoo management and design. The book collection grows at a rate of 150 items annually. A collection development policy guides subject emphasis and intensity. Conference proceedings, workshop papers, and research reports of sister zoological gardens are actively sought and comprise an important part of the overall collection.

Over 300 periodical titles are received annually by subscription, gift and exchange. One hundred are paid subscriptions, one-fifth of which are medical and veterinary journals. *Current Contents: Agriculture, Biology, and Environmental Sciences* is routed to zoo staff as a weekly current awareness tool. *Wildlife Disease Review, Wildlife Review, Animal Behavior Abstracts*, and *Zoological Record* are available in the library. Four titles are received specific to the profession of zoo keeping: *Animal Keepers Forum* (American Association of Zoo Keepers), *Ratel* (Association of British Wild Animal Keepers), *Thylacinus* (Australasian Society of Zoo Keepers) and *Zoo Biology*. Studbooks, periodic compilations of animal parentage and location, are another resource maintained by the library.[7]

SPECIAL COLLECTIONS

The library maintains four distinct special collections: the Zoo and Aquarium Reference Collection (ZARC), the Zoo Poster Collection, the Lincoln Park Archives, and an audio-visual collection.[8]

Three of these collections owe their creation to Walter Necker. In his progress report, he recommended the establishment of special collections as a way to give the library a unique character. He recognized the importance of preserving the history of both Lincoln Park Zoo and other national and international zoos. ZARC is a general zoological garden archive. Information on over 200 worldwide zoos is collected and held by the library. The bulk of materials is comprised of guidebooks, maps, newsletters, animal inventories, annual reports and promotional materials. Graphic representations of other zoos are maintained in the Zoo Poster Collection. Published art works from over sixty national and international zoos are owned by the library. Posters are framed and displayed in the library and other administrative offices.

The Lincoln Park Zoo Archives are the largest and most significant of the special collections. Documents cover the beginning of Lincoln Park in the mid-1800s to the present. Annual reports, correspondence, daily log books, scrapbooks (dating from 1922), post cards, buttons, collectibles and memorabilia are owned. A public catalog consisting of photocopies of annual reports of the zoo (1889-) and Lincoln Park Zoological Society (1960-) allows for complete public access to a comprehensive research tool while protecting original documents.[9]

The Audiovisual Collection consists of over 400 video cassettes. Tapes include keeper training workshops, lectures, films of animal activities (arrivals, departures, introductions, births) and medical procedures. A major component of the video collection is a set (204 tapes) of former zoo director Marlin Perkins' "Zoo Parade," a television show filmed live at Lincoln Park Zoo from May 1949 to September 1957.

SERVICES

The library's primary purpose is supporting the information needs of zoo personnel, zoological society members and the general public. Its services are designed to further the goals of the zoo, to educate the public and to promote the exchange of scientific information. Specific public services are performed to meet the information needs of these many users.

The librarian conducts literature searches and provides bibliographic instruction at the request of zoo personnel. When necessary, the librarian visits libraries with larger and more comprehensive collections for additional resources. Professional contacts at local universities and special libraries occasionally provide free database searching for zoo staff. Zoo personnel also make use of the library's interlibrary loan service. A member of ILLINET (Illinois Library and Information Network), the library has access via interlibrary loan to a wealth of materials throughout the city and state.

Society members and the general public are served in person, by telephone and through letters. Many of the inquiries received by the office switchboard are channeled to the library for assistance. All letters arriving at Lincoln Park Zoo from school children are forwarded to the library. Non-staff library users make appointments for access to the library and are assisted by the librarian. The library averages thirteen calls and visitors a day.

The librarian prepares specialized subject bibliographies to supplement zoo programs. Reading lists based on the library's collections are provided to members who travel on Society sponsored "safaris" and for members who attend the quarterly "Zoo Lecture Series" organized by the zoo's Education Department. In the last four years, twenty-one bibliographies have been written covering such subjects as zoo design, peregrine falcons, gorillas, and Madagascar. Copies of these lists are offered free of charge to other zoos, as well.

The librarian selects and reviews books for the *Lincoln Park Zoo Review*, a quarterly news publication for the members of the Lincoln Park Zoological Society. Generally books are popular and nontechnical in subject matter and available for purchase in the zoo's Gift Shop.[10]

IMS CONSERVATION PROJECT

According to the tenets of AAZPA, conservation is one of the four goals of zoological gardens. The conservation ethic, nurturing a responsible attitude toward wildlife and nature, has become a compelling philosophical force in the world of zoos. Today, zoos are the protectors and propagators of their living collections, endangered species.

Libraries, however, also have collections they must conserve. When Lincoln Park Zoo Library received a conservation grant from the Institute of Museum Services (IMS) in 1986, it was an acknowledgement of the commitment to conserve these nonliving collections.

Archival documents, as rare as beautiful snow leopards, were mishandled and stored haphazardly; not so much from lack of caring, but more from lack of knowledge of proper care and environmentally safe storage. The grant from IMS gave funds for two consultants from the Northeast Document Conservation Center. Before their arrival, over one hundred boxes of documents were superficially cleaned and relocated to a better storage site. Next, individual items were selected for examination based on their condition and value to the overall collection including glass plate negatives, loose photographs, scrapbooks, blueprints, animal X rays, books, ledgers, and loose correspondence.

George Martin Cunha performed an environmental site survey. Gary Albright examined the photographic and print materials and made recommendations for their care. Their reports provided the information necessary to pursue a total and continuing archival conservation program. The nonliving collections of Lincoln Park Zoo can now be protected and preserved.[11]

ZOO 2000

Zoos, in recognizing the demands of scientific investigation, have begun slowly formalizing their dissemination of information. In the early years, information was circulated among zoos by a confederation of zoo directors and curators. Insights, tips, and new methods in animal management were passed on by correspondence, telephone conversations, visits and meetings. Zoological information was scattered in an array of journals covering many disciplines — general biology, veterinary and human medicine, ecology, behavior, physiology, and others. When reports were published, reprints were exchanged among colleagues. Instead of institutions building libraries, individuals with a bibliographical bent owned sizable personal libraries. These private collections, even if generously shared by their owners, were not open to a wide range of users, and, as a result, restricted the accessibility of information.

In 1959, the Zoological Society of London issued *International Zoo Yearbook* (IZY), a landmark publication in the zoo world. Written specifically for zoo professionals and published annually, *IZY* contains a potpourri of zoo management information. Volume 24/25 (1986) includes a section on captive breeding of endangered species, a section on "New Developments in the Zoo World," and a handy reference section listing international zoos and aquaria, a census of rare animals in captivity, studbooks and their compilers, etc. The Zoological Society of London stands true to its 1826 purpose of "advancing the science of zoology."

The rapid growth in zoological literature is a challenge for zoo librarians. New groups and programs are created constantly, with each publishing a newsletter, conference proceedings, or animal management papers. Newsletters which change title, numbering, and period of publication may become the significant scientific journal of 2001. Important meetings, held at a different zoo each year, produce papers which could revolutionize animal management. These critically important works, usually printed privately and never found in standard indices, are the illusive prey of zoo librarians. Working in concert with zoos and similar organizations which have taken the role of small publisher, the zoo librarian can insure that information not be lost in the abyss of documentation.

Research programs in zoos are expanding.[12] This increase in scientific activity is the final step toward the changing of a menagerie into a scientific institution. Progress in the standardization of animal management techniques and practices creates the demand for standardized ways to transfer information and records. Today, zoos manage the internal and external explosion of information in several ways. Internationally, ISIS (International Species Inventory System) maintains animal records. ARKS (Animal Record Keeping System) is a newly developed computer program for zoos. International counterparts, such as the British system known as NOAH (National On-line Animal History), are in the works. The 3" by 5" index card method suggested by Caroline Jarvis in 1969 is rapidly becoming a computer printout.[13]

In 1965, Ronald T. Reuter, Cleveland Zoo assistant director, presented his colleagues with the future of zoo libraries when he said " . . . it is not unrealistic to assume that a central zoology library operated with modern electronic techniques could be the reservoir from which zoos . . . could call for (such) information to be flashed on a TV screen mounted at their respective locations in a matter of seconds."[14] By 1981, AAZPA Executive Director, Robert Wagner, wrote "libraries are an increasing important part of zoos and aquariums . . ."[15] Quickly developing as partners in information management, zoo and aquarium libraries are, however, relatively new entities in the world of zoos and special libraries.[16]

Information professionals in zoos are taking on many roles and are partners in the exchange of information among zoos.[17] They are not only developing collections of books and journals to assist in day-to-day information needs, but they can use their expertise in managing rapid changes in information technology. Librarians can work with developers of zoo computer systems lending experience and knowledge in data base management and use. Information professionals should insure that Zoo 2000 is a totally integrated information system.

STATISTICS

Name of Zoo:	Lincoln Park Zoological Gardens Chicago, Illinois
Date Founded:	1868
Name of Library: Reference Library	Lincoln Park Zoological Gardens
Telephone:	312/294-4640
Name of Library Director:	Joyce M. Shaw, Zoo Librarian
Library Collection Size	
Number of Monographs:	2,000
Number of Bound Journals:	450
Number of Subscriptions:	300
Other:	Special Collections
Main Subjects Collected:	Zoology, veterinary medicine, conservation biology, zoo management and design
Staff Size:	1 professional 4 volunteers
Online searching done:	No

Interlibrary loans made: Yes
Names of network affiliations: ILLINET, Chicago Library System, AAZPA Library Interest Group

REFERENCE NOTES

1. Hill, Clyde H. Zoo. *World Book Encyclopedia*. 21:505; 1978.
2. Conway, William G. Zoo and aquarium philosophy. *In*: Sausman, Karen, ed. *Zoological park and aquarium fundamentals*. Wheeling, West Virginia: American Association of Zoological Parks and Aquariums; 1982: pp. 3-12.
3. *Annual Report of the Commissioners of Lincoln Park*. (year ending) March 31, 1869. Chicago: Commissioners of Lincoln Park, 1869: p. 51.
4. Bryan, I. J. (compiler). *Report of the Commissioners and a history of Lincoln Park*. Chicago: Commissioners of Lincoln Park, 1899: pp. 76-84.
5. Shaw, Joyce M. *Collection size of zoo and aquarium libraries*. November 1983, p. 4. (manuscript).
6. Necker, Walter L. *Report of the Library Consultant to the Lincoln Park Zoological Gardens through September 1979*. p. 6 (manuscript).
7. Glatston, Angela R. Studbooks: the basis of breeding programs. *International Zoo Yearbook*. 24/25: 162-167; 1986.
8. Shaw, Joyce M. Lincoln Park Zoo Library: an introduction to the library and its special collections. *Illinois Libraries*. 66(4): 164-166; 1984 April.
9. Jurgens, Jane Catherine. In the stacks. *Origins*. 2(1): 3-4; 1985 November.
10. Shaw, Joyce M. Zoo book reviews: Safari guides for the spirited traveler. *Lincoln Park Zoo Review*. 2(2): 11; 1987 Summer.
11. Shaw, Joyce M. Lions and tigers and bears: a report on the Lincoln Park Zoo Archives. *Museum Archivist*. 2(1): 5-6; 1987 December.
12. Finlay, Ted W., Maple, Terry L. A survey of research in American zoos and aquariums. *Zoo Biology*. 5(3): 261-168; 1985.
13. Jarvis, Caroline. Studying wild mammals in captivity: standard life histories with an appendix on zoo records. *International Zoo Yearbook*. 9:316-328; 1969.
14. Reuter, Ronald T. Recent zoological literature. *AAZPA 67th Annual Conference Proceedings*. Wheeling, West Virginia; American Association of Zoological Parks and Aquariums; 1965; pp. z47-z51.
15. Wagner, Robert. Executive director report. *AAZPA Newsletter*. XXII (5): p. 3; 1981 May.
16. Kenyon, Kay A. Zoo/aquarium libraries: a survey. *Special Libraries*. 65(4): 329-334; 1984 October.
17. Rost, Alan F. A survey of recent developments in zoological information management. *AAZPA Annual Conference Proceedings*. Wheeling, West Virginia: American Association of Zoological Parks and Aquariums; 1985; pp. 389-392.

APPENDIX A

Zoo libraries are as difficult to find in the literature as the giant panda is to track in the wild. The following is a bibliography of articles relating to libraries and information services in zoos and aquariums. It is by no means complete, and the author welcomes additions.

ZOO AND AQUARIUM LIBRARIES: A BIBLIOGRAPHY

Black, J.; Curtis, L. The research program at Oklahoma City Zoo. *Oklahoma City Zoo Journal*. 5(1): 9-10 (and appendix E); 1981 June.

Davies, Denise. The challenge of zoo and aquarium libraries. *Biofeedback*. 10(4): 4-5; 1984 Summer.

Jurgens, Jane C. In the stacks. *Origins*. 2(1): 3-4; 1985 November.

Kaufman, Ron. A voice from the volumes. *Zoo* (Topeka Zoo). 17(2): unpaged; 1981.

Kenyon, Kay A. Spotlight on: National Zoological Park Library. *Biofeedback*. 12(4): 4-5; 1987 Winter.

Kenyon, Kay A. Zoo/aquarium libraries; a survey. *Special Libraries*. 75(4): 329-334; 1984 October.

Local librarians donate vacation time. *Tulsa Zoo News*. July/August: 6; 1984.

Powers, Jan. John G. Shedd Aquarium Library. *Science & Technology Libraries*. 6(1/2): 83-89; 1985-86 Fall-Winter.

Quinn, Kathy. When in doubt, look it up. *Animaland* (Staten Island Zoological Society). 52(1): 13; 1987.

Reuter, Ronald T. Recent zoological literature. *AAZPA 67th Annual conference Proceedings*. Wheeling, West Virginia: American Association of Zoological Parks and Aquariums; 1965; pp. Z47-Z51.

Robinson, Michaele M. Spotlight on The Ernst Schwarz Library of the Zoological Society of San Diego. *Biofeedback*. 12(3): 10-11; 1986.

Rost, Alan F. Every zoo can have one—the zoo library. *AAZPA 1984 Regional Conference Proceedings*. Wheeling, West Virginia: American Association of Zoological Parks and Aquariums; 1984: pp. 269-272.

Rost, Alan F. A survey of recent developments in zoological information management. *AAZPA Annual Conference Proceedings*. Wheeling, West Virginia: American Association of Zoological Parks and Aquariums; 1985; pp. 389-392.

Roti Roti, Donna. Aquatic science center library, John G. Shedd Aquarium. *Illinois Libraries*. 62(3): 264-267; 1980 March.

Ryan, Kathleen; Kenyon, Kay. Zoological libraries. *Sci-Tech News*. 38(2): 33-34; 1984 April.

Sabol, Cathy. Kay Kenyon: Zoo librarian provides animal answers. *American Libraries*. 17(4): 285; 1986 April.

Shaw, Joyce M. Lincoln Park Zoo Library; an introduction to the library and its special collections. *Illinois Libraries*. 66(4): 164-166; 1984 April.

Shaw, Joyce M. Lions and tigers and bears: a report on the Lincoln Park Zoo Archives. *Museum Archives*. 2(1): 5-6; 1987 December.
Weiss, Cathy. The zoo library. *Zoosounds* (Oklahoma Zoological Society). 4-5; 1987 Summer.
Zabel, Jean. Librarynews. *Zooming In* (Milwaukee County Zoo). unpaged; 1981 May.

New York Zoological Society Library

Steven P. Johnson

SUMMARY. The institutional setting, clientele, collecting policies, collections, services and history of the New York Zoological Society Library are discussed. The diverse activities and divisions of the institution are described.

INSTITUTIONAL SETTING

The New York Zoological Society (NYZS) was chartered by the State of New York in 1895 for the purpose of founding and operating a zoological park and facilitating original research in zoology and related subjects and for the instruction and recreation of the people. The Bronx Zoo, formally known as the New York Zoological Park (NYZP) and located in the southern part of Bronx Park, opened in 1899. In 1902, the Society assumed management of the municipally operated New York Aquarium, then located in Castle Garden at Battery Park in Manhattan. Currently (1987), NYZS consists of five operating divisions. In addition to the zoo and the aquarium, the divisions are the Osborn Laboratories of Marine Sciences, located adjacent to the New York Aquarium at Coney Island in Brooklyn, the Wildlife Survival Center and Wildlife Conservation International (WCI). The Wildlife Survival Center specializes in breeding endangered species in nonexhibit facilities. WCI, one of the oldest nongovernmental wildlife conservation programs in the world, traces its origin to the Zoological Society's sponsorship of a wildlife survey of Alaska in 1896. In recent years, WCI has

---

Steven P. Johnson is Supervising Librarian/Archivist at the New York Zoological Society. He earned an MA in Library Science and MA in History at the University of Wisconsin-Madison and specializes in database searching and archives management.

© 1988 by The Haworth Press, Inc. All rights reserved.

supported more than 50 projects in more than 30 countries, annually.

Activities not obviously suggested by these divisions include the publication of the bimonthly magazine *Animal Kingdom* (circulation, 155,000) and the New York City Zoos Project, which will reopen Central Park Zoo and other New York City Parks Department zoos under NYZS management. The library of the New York Zoological Society supports the library service requirements of these divisions to varying degrees, with a few major exceptions. For example, a separate, independently managed library is maintained at the Osborn Laboratories of Marine Sciences, located at the New York Aquarium. As a result the NYZS Library provides minimal services to the Aquarium and the Osborn Laboratories. The archival component of the NYZS library program serves the Zoological Society as a whole.[1]

The NYZS library is operated primarily for the staff of the New York Zoological Society. In addition to stack access and loan privileges, services provided to NYZS staff include a current awareness service based on contents pages of selected current journals, database searching using Dialog, Wilsearch and other systems and interlibrary loans. In general, no charges are imposed on department budgets for database searches or interlibrary services.

In addition to directors, curators, educators, artists, animal keepers and other staff of the Bronx Zoo, users of NYZS library collections and services include staff of *Animal Kingdom* magazine, visiting zoo curators, zoologists and other researchers, and college and other students from the metropolitan New York area. In part because of the library's location in the Administration Building of the Bronx Zoo, zoo staff represent the largest percentage of the library users.

Nonresident staff, however, also use the library's collections and services. For example, current facilities of the Wildlife Survival Center are located at St. Catherine's Island off the Georgia coast. Library services are provided to Survival Center staff by mail, telephone and by occasionally by computer disk or modem. A facsimile machine link with the Wildlife Survival Center should be in place by Spring 1988. Survival Center staff also use the library during their periodic visits to the Bronx Zoo.

Field researchers from Wildlife Conservation International (WCI) represent another category of nonresident library users. Although WCI is headquartered at the zoo, few WCI staff are in residence. Permanent and project zoologists usually reside at the site of field projects scattered around the world. Visiting zoologists often use the NYZS library and archival records derived from past field work. The limited duration of stateside visits sometimes means that field researchers cannot conveniently visit comprehensive research libraries such as the library of the American Museum of Natural History, the largest zoology library in the northeastern United States (and western hemisphere).

Members of the Zoological Society, students and other researchers and members of the public may request appointments to use the library on a time and space available basis. Telephone reference service to the public is generally limited to holdings verification, directory type data, and historical information.

COLLECTIONS

Vertebrate zoology, management of wildlife in captivity, wildlife conservation and veterinary medicine are the main subjects collected. Veterinary medicine is represented mainly by journal literature. Hamer's 1982 description of literature for zoo libraries was based largely on NYZS library holdings.[2]

The monograph collection consists of about 5,000 volumes, with annual acquisitions of about 100 volumes plus volumes published in series. The monograph collection emphasizes endangered species and animal species which are or were in the collections of the Bronx Zoo.

About two hundred journals are received on a subscription or exchange basis, representing more than two-thirds of the acquisition budget. Almost half of these titles are received in exchange for *Animal Kingdom* and the NYZS annual report. This total of two hundred titles does not include the dozens of zoo and conservation organization newsletters and annual reports which arrive with no acquisitions effort. Zoo and organization materials are filed according to name of organization or location of zoo or aquarium, but are not checked in or claimed.

Books are cataloged in-house according to modified Anglo-American Cataloging Rules, second edition, and classified according to Library of Congress schedules interpreted to favor classification in the taxonomic rather than geographic or discipline sections. Journals are not cataloged or classified, but a current journals list is updated once or twice per year. The journals list is available on request.

Among important titles in the serials collection are complete or near complete sets of *Zoological Record, Der Zoologische Garten, Proceedings of the Zoological Society of London/Journal of Zoology, Journal of the Bombay Natural History Society, East African Wildlife Society Journal/African Journal of Ecology, Aviculture* and *Auk*. Recently, historical data on shipments of animals between zoos in Europe and the United States, published in *Proceedings of the Zoological Society of London* and *Der Zoologische Garten*, has been used in research and planning for the Species Survival Plan (SSP) of the American Association of Zoological Parks and Aquariums.

Substantial, though largely uncataloged departmental library collections are maintained by the Animal Health Center, Department of Publications and Department of Education. A portion of the cataloged ornithology collection, particularly older works, is maintained in Ornithology Department offices. The library of the former Tropical Research Department and Tropical Research Station, has been integrated into the main library collection.

HISTORY OF THE COLLECTION AND FACILITIES

The NYZS library began as an office collection maintained by Bronx Zoo director William Hornaday, who later donated many books and personal papers to the Society. In 1908 the Society erected an administration building in the zoo. The second floor of the building included a library reading room and a stacks room, comparable to current facilities.[3]

Executive Committee Chairman Madison Grant summarized the collection policy of the new library in 1910. Noting that the Society had no desire to establish a library "of value only to systematists," he pointed out the "strong demand for what may well be called a library of practical zoological knowledge, developed with especial reference to the actual needs of the public."[4]

In 1916, Grant presented a plan to "secure $5,000 for the purchase of books and periodicals especially devoted to the conservation of wild life throughout the world. . . . A complete conservation library," he wrote, "would be of great service to the great cause of wild life protection."[5] Apparently, this fund was never raised, but conservation literature did become an area of collection strength.

Five years later, writing to Henry Fairfield Osborn, president of both the American Museum of Natural History and the New York Zoological Society, Bronx Zoo director William Hornaday elaborated on the need to limit the NYZS library collection to literature of practical value to the staff of the zoo. Pointing out that the AMNH library was the "centre of zoological literature for New York City and . . . likely to remain so" Hornaday proposed that the NYZS library limit its journal exchange program to English language materials in vertebrate zoology and purchase nonEnglish language materials only as needed.[6] The Executive Committee subsequently adopted this policy.[7]

Initially, librarians were engaged for short-term periods to catalog collections; a permanent, full-time librarian did not join the staff until 1970. Zoo librarians and archivists since that time have included Tsung S. Su, 1970-1972, Arline Schneider, 1972-1975, Allegra Hamer, 1975-1982, George Utting, library assistant and assistant archivist, 1978-1980, and Terry Collins, archivist, 1980-1981.

From about 1940 until 1970, the library collections were dispersed throughout curatorial and other offices and halls of the administration building. Since 1970, the library has occupied a reading room on the first floor of the administration building. The archives room and library stacks rooms are located in the administration building basement. Since 1976, initially as a result of the

New York City fiscal crisis, the library reading room has also been the location of the animal records and shipping department.

SPECIAL COLLECTIONS

Special collections materials at NYZS fall into two categories: materials requiring "special care" due to age, physical condition or any other reason and institutional archives. The "special care" category is relatively small, compared to the archives. "Special care" materials include limited edition and other difficult to replace books, paintings and sculpture and a collection of books by present and past staff members.

The institutional archives currently consist of about 900 linear feet of records dating from the earliest years of the Zoological Society to the present. The archives include the noncurrent records of enduring value of each of the Zoological Society's present and former operating divisions. Although the bulk of the archives are unpublished material, the archives also include record sets of institutional publications. These publications include annual reports, the scientific quarterly *Zoologica* (which suspended publication after volume 58, 1973) and the *Bulletin of the New York Zoological Society*, which changed title to *Animal Kingdom* in 1942.

Most use of the unpublished archives has been by or for NYZS staff. The archives have been used intensively for several "outside" research projects, however. The librarian regularly uses the archives to respond to historical reference queries from the public.

Retired NYZS curator William Bridges drew on the archival correspondence of Bronx Zoo director William Hornaday in *Gathering of Animals: an unconventional history of the New York Zoological Society*, the official history of NYZS, published in 1974.[1] Later, following the official organization of the archives, the archives were a major source for Martha Hill's biographical study of Carl Rungius, published in 1984,[8] and *Carl Rungius: painter of the western wilderness* by Jon Whyte and E. J. Hart, published in 1985.[9]

Organization of the archives began in the early 1970s, with interest spurred by the 75th anniversary of the zoo in 1974. The H. W. Wilson Foundation provided initial funding for work on the archives by library staff in 1977 and 1978. The continued support of the H. W. Wilson Foundation led, in 1979, to the formal establishment of the archives and a one-year archives preservation program undertaken jointly with the neighboring New York Botanical Garden Library. The National Historical Publications and Records Commission (NHPRC) provided outright and matching grant funds for this project, under which records were surveyed, brought together in a new facility and inventoried. One product of this project was *Guide to the Archives of the New York Zoological Society*, printed in 1982 and available on request.[10] Subsequently, the guide was submitted to the New York State Historical Documents Inventory, based at Cornell University, which used the guide as a source of entries for the Bronx county archives inventory and for submission to the Research Libraries Network database (RLIN).[11]

STAFFING AND ORGANIZATIONAL SETTING

The library is staffed by a full-time librarian/archivist and by one or more part-time assistants, often students from the nearby Bronx campus of Fordham University. The librarian/archivist reports to the registrar, a curator in charge of the Animal Services Department of the Bronx Zoo. The registrar in turn reports to the general curator of the Bronx Zoo. In addition to the librarian, Animal Services Department personnel consist of a zoologist, zoological assistant and a shipping clerk, who maintain animal records, obtain import and export permits, make shipping and receiving arrangements for living collections of the zoo and compile studbook data for Species Survival Plan (SSP) species. A recent addition to the Animal Services Department staff is a full-time conservation biologist, charged with coordinating and promoting original research using the living collections of the zoo, including screening and fulfilling requests for biological materials.

The close association of the library and animal records functions at NYZS reflects a pattern which is relatively common among medium-sized zoos in the United States.

COMPUTER APPLICATIONS

Current computer-supported library applications include original cataloging and card printing (Bibbase-Cat, Small Library Computing); current journals list, exchange list, interlibrary loan log, art collection inventory and archives inventories (dbase III, recently converted from dbase II); subject heading authority list, zoo and conservation organization newsletter and annual report authority file, archives accession log and correspondence (Wordstar). Procomm is used for modem access to Dialog, the Metropolitan Interlibrary Cooperative System (MILCS), MCI mail, Easylink, other networks and bulletin boards. Computer applications in varying stages of planning include a bibliography based on the BITS current awareness system from Biosis, Inc., retrospective conversion of the card catalog to machine readable form and establishment of computerized public catalog.

Library and archives computer hardware consists of an IBM PC with 30 megabyte hard disk, 3.5" and 5.25" floppy disk drives, dot matrix printer and modem. Portable and other staff-owned equipment is often used for data entry in the archives and other locations remote from the library computer station.

The latest hardware addition to the library is a facsimile machine. Although it will primarily be used to facilitate animal shipping and import-export permit applications, the fax machine should be useful in library applications as well. For example, the New York Regional Medical Library will fill photocopy requests via facsimile for a small premium over normal service charges.

RELATIONSHIPS WITH OTHER LIBRARIES

The American Museum of Natural History (AMNH) Library has influenced the collecting policy of the NYZS library since its founding, due to the comprehensive nature of the AMNH Library collections in zoology and natural history. From an early date, NYZS determined not to duplicate the holdings of AMNH. Although travel to the Museum Library, located in Manhattan, is not convenient for most zoo staff—travel requires at least an hour in each direction—the availability of interlibrary loans from the Museum provides reliable access to virtually any zoological literature not held locally.

The New York Botanical Garden (NYBG) library, located in the northern part of Bronx Park, is one of the world's largest botany and horticulture libraries. As neighboring institutions with a shared status as state chartered New York City cultural institutions, NYBG and NYZS have cooperated in major and minor projects for decades. Examples of library cooperation include cataloging provided under contract by NYBG to NYZS in the early 1970s, the joint employment of archives program staff from 1979 to 1982 and occasional joint purchases of library and archives supplies. The growing importance of zoo horticulture in recent years has increased the use of NYBG library collections by NYZS staff. To a large degree, the close proximity of the NYBG Library has relieved the NYZS library of the responsibility to collect horticultural works. The NYZS librarian and staff regularly use the Botanical Garden Library's extensive collection of biological and natural history journals and first rate reference collection.

To facilitate cooperation with other aquarium and zoo libraries, the NYZS library participates in the Librarian's Special Interest Group (LSIG) of the American Association of Zoological Parks and Aquariums. LSIG publishes a newsletter, bibliographies and core lists of monographs and journals for aquarium and zoo libraries.

In order to structure relations with the broader universe of libraries, the NYZS library participates in the New York City Metropolitan Research and Reference Library Agency (METRO). METRO provides member libraries with access to the New York State Library and New York State Interlibrary Loan System, an annual directory of member libraries in the METRO region, a regional serials union list and free dialup access to the New York Library Online Network (LION) database, among other services.

STATISTICS

Parent institution	New York Zoological Society
Name of Zoo	New York Zoological Park; better known as Bronx Zoo
Founded	1895; opened, 1899
Name of library	New York Zoological Society Library

Telephone number 212 220-6874
Facsimile number 212 220-7114
MCI name and ID number New York Zoological Society; 294-6915
Easylink mailbox number 62953759
Name of library director Steven P. Johnson
Staff size Professional: 1.0
 Clerical: 0.5
Library collection size
 Number of monographs 5,000
 Number of bound journals 2,100; 28 current titles regularly bound
 Current subscriptions 200
Main subjects collected Vertebrate zoology, mangement of wild animals in captivity, wildlife conservation and veterinary
Online searching Yes, staff only
Interlibrary loans made Yes
Networks New York Metropolitan Reference and Research Library Agency (METRO); American Association of Zoological Parks and Aquariums Librarians Special Interest Group; Museum Archives Roundtable, Society of American Archivists.

NOTES

1. Bridges, William. *Gathering of animals: an unconventional history of the New York Zoological Society*. New York: Harper; 1974. New York Zoological Society. *Annual report, 1986-87*. Bronx: The Society, [1987].

2. Hamer, Allegra. Zoological literature. *In*: Kent, Allen; Daily, Jay E., eds. *Encyclopedia of library and information sciences*. New York: Marcel Dekker; 1982. 33: 529-544.

3. New York Zoological Society. *Thirteenth annual report . . . 1908*. Bronx: The Society; 1909: page 39. New York Zoological Society. *Fourteenth annual report . . . 1909*. Bronx: The Society; 1910: pages 39-40.

4. New York Zoological Society. *Fifteenth annual report . . . 1910*. Bronx: The Society; 1911: page 43.

5. New York Zoological Society. *Twenty-first annual report . . . 1916*. Bronx: The Society; 1917: pages 47-48.

6. Hornaday, William, to Henry Fairfield Osborn. [Letterpress copy.] 1921 February 3. 1 leaf. New York Zoological Society Archives, Bronx, NY; Record Group 5, New York Zoological Park, Director's Office records, outgoing correspondence, vol. 44: 537.

7. New York Zoological Society. Executive Committee. Extracts from minutes of the 280th meeting . . . 1921 February 10th. 1 leaf. New York Zoological Society Archives, Bronx, NY; Record Group 5, New York Zoological Park, Director's office records, incoming correspondence; box 72, folder 6.

8. Hill, Martha. For purple mountain majesties. *Audubon.* 86: 57-63; 1984 November.

9. Whyte, Jon; Hart, E.J. *Carl Rungius: painter of the western wilderness.* Vancouver/Toronto: The Glenbow-Alberta Institute; Douglas & McIntyre; 1985.

10. Collins, Terry; Hamer, Allegra. Archives programs for zoological parks and aquariums. *In: AAZPA regional conference proceedings 1981.* [Wheeling, West Virginia]: American Association of Zoological Parks and Aquariums; 1982: 99-102.

11. New York Zoological Society. *Guide to the archives of the New York Zoological Society.* Compiled by Terry Collins and Steven P. Johnson. Bronx, NY: The Society; 1982.

Zoological Society of San Diego Library

Michaele M. Robinson

SUMMARY. Describes the providing of corporate information services to a zoological organization of 1,200 employees located in two facilities. Discusses the history and development of the library collections, and the services provided to users.

ZOOLOGICAL SOCIETY OF SAN DIEGO

The Zoological Society of San Diego is a private nonprofit corporation that operates two animal facilities under its jurisdiction: the 125-acre San Diego Zoo and the San Diego Wild Animal Park, an 1,800-acre park located thirty miles to the north.

It is often said that the San Diego Zoo "began with a roar." One day in 1916, physician Harry M. Wegeforth was driving past the animal cages of the Panama-California International Exposition in Balboa Park when he heard one of the lions roar. He turned to his brother and said, "Wouldn't it be splendid if San Diego had a zoo! You know . . . I think I'll start one."

Soon after Wegeforth's comment to his brother, a small board of directors was formed, and the first official meeting of the Zoological Society of San Diego was held October 2, 1916. On the following November 24, the Articles of Incorporation were sent to the State of California for approval; included in them was a provision for a scientific research library. "Dr. Harry," as he was called by his staff, wanted a good research program for the Zoo. In 1927, with funds provided by San Diego benefactress Ellen Browning Scripps, the Zoo's first hospital was built. A small medical library located on its main floor was to be the first of many locations of the Zoo's library. The majority of research conducted at the hospital

---

Michaele M. Robinson has a BA in English from San Diego State University. She is Manager of Library Services for the Zoological Society of San Diego, P.O. Box 551, San Diego, CA 92112-0551.

during those early years involved comparative medicine. Among the investigations of the 1930s and 1940s were studies on polio virus, poultry diseases, and primate retinas. Books and journals were purchased by researchers and housed in the hospital's library. Early photos of the library show it complete with wingback chairs and a fireplace. Volunteer librarians classified these materials from time to time, but there was no formal library arrangement.

In 1954, an administration building was completed which included a board of directors' room/library. This was the beginning of the Zoo's natural history library. In 1960, a part-time librarian was hired for what was then a collection of about 500 volumes. By 1964 the librarian's job was full-time. In 1966, the library moved to the newly completed education building. Although plans for the library originally began with 6,000 sq. ft., the space finally allocated was only 500 sq. ft. A few moves later, in October 1983, the library was relocated once again, this time to 2,000 sq. ft. in a warehouse. For the first time, space for study tables was available, also a technical services room, a special collections room, and office space for the librarian and assistant, along with stack space for the nearly 9,000 volumes the main library had acquired.

By now, the original hospital library had been converted to several offices and a conference room. Its collection of books and journals told the story of the various researchers who came and went. Several years' run of virology journals ended with the departure of the virologist. Then began five or six years of tropical medicine journals, again terminating when the scientist left the staff. In 1978, with the completion of a new clinical wing in the hospital compound, a small medical library was included. This facility currently includes a collection of 2,500 volumes of zoological medicine materials and serves a research and clinical staff of over 50 individuals.

ERNST SCHWARZ

Ernst Schwarz was a noted mammalian taxonomist. Among the animals for which he provided systematic treatments were the pygmy chimpanzee, the hartebeests, the colobus monkeys, lemurs, mangabeys, and the now-extinct Bali tiger. Through his long-time association with the Zoo, Schwarz provided his expertise to the staff for many years. After his death in 1961, his widow donated his books and reprint collection to the Zoo's library, and on July 21, 1976, the library was officially dedicated as the Ernst Schwarz Library. The Schwarz collection formed the core of the natural history collection.

Another major building block of the natural history collection was the receipt of the herpetological library of Charles E. Shaw, the Zoo's former curator of reptiles, who died in 1970.

The 1970s saw the growth of the horticulture departments at each campus and, consequently, the addition of two horticulture libraries.

MAIN LIBRARY AND SATELLITES

By the mid-1980s, the Zoological Society had grown to include two animal parks: the San Diego Zoo and the San Diego Wild Animal Park, which opened in 1972. A combined employee population of 1,200 permanent staff members is needed to operate the two facilities. To provide optimum library services for this large number of people, with their various disciplines, and the added problem of two locations, the organization of library services includes a main natural history library, located at the Zoo, and several satellite collections. The medical library is located in the Zoo's Jennings Center for Zoological Medicine. A horticulture library of approximately 500 volumes is housed in the Zoo's horticulture offices. The library at the Wild Animal Park, though mainly dealing with horticulture, holds more than 2,000 volumes and is located in a temporary trailer. All of the satellite libraries have a card catalog, with the main library's catalog being the master catalog. Several departments have book collections as well, including the education department, graphics, architecture, development, public relations, and the curators.

SERVICES, STAFF, OPERATIONS

The main library is the operations center for all. It is also the only one that is staffed. Two full-time employees are responsible for providing library/information services to the entire organization.

Combined holdings have grown from that group of a few hundred books in 1960 to exceed 10,000 books and 5,000 bound journals, with 605 periodical titles received annually. Also included are 10,000 reprints and pamphlets on vertebrate zoology; a collection of zoo newsletters, guidebooks, and annual reports; a staff publication file; map file; microform collection; and the archives. The latter include an oral history program with 78 audio and video tapes to date, curators' and keepers' diaries, newspaper clippings dating from the Zoo's early days in 1916, and a biography file of former and current institution officials and staff.

Subject interests include vertebrate zoology, zoogeography, animal husbandry, animal behavior, wildlife conservation and ecology, zoological medicine, and horticulture. The library includes a collection of animal studbooks which are used for collection management. The International Species Inventory System (ISIS), which systematically lists information on individual specimens exhibited at various zoos, is used to pair unmated animals for genetic balance, trade, or disposition. A collection of zoo master plans and exhibits is used for research and exhibit planning. In addition to containing the archives, the special collections room holds the rare book collection of rare or out-of-print materials. Many of these contain hand-colored plates by wildlife artists such as Kuelemans, Smit, Gronvold, Wolf, Jardine, Ridgway, and Thorburn.

The library's primary responsibility, or mission, is to provide library/information services to support the research, exhibition of animals and plants, specialized staff interests, and the general goals of the organization. The principal users of these services are the curators, keepers, veterinarians, research personnel, and educators. However, support must also be there for gardeners, sign illustrators, food service personnel, public relations writers, and technicians and administrators at all levels. The library also helps outside writers and scholars, graduate students, and the general public.

One of the services provided is in the form of information packages on new or expected animals. It started as a form of self-defense, after having reinvented the wheel for the sixth or seventh time for a curator or keeper asking for material on new animals. These information packages became so popular that the practice has now become a proactive way whereby the library provides well-researched and authoritative information on new exhibit animals to anyone and everyone in the organization. Material usually included is the animal's natural history, including habitat and bioclimatic information, husbandry, nutrition requirements, and illustrations — a somewhat customized bibliography. The librarian attends exhibit-planning meetings to gather information on which animals will be included in new exhibits so that the animal packages can be prepared well in advance of their need.

The library has been a member of OCLC for two years. Cataloging of books and interlibrary loan transactions are conducted through OCLC. As anticipated, the interlibrary loan volume has increased markedly since the library has been able to fill requests faster and with much more success.

Several computerized literature searches per month are conducted using DIALOG and OCLC Link. Major data bases used are ZOOLOGICAL RECORD, BIOSIS, MEDLINE, and CAB ABSTRACTS.

Tables of contents of journals are routed routinely to staff as a current awareness service. A monthly newsletter with acquisitions is distributed as well. Every new employee is given a copy of the library's guide to information services.

This year several natural history videotapes were added to the collection. They have become very popular with the staff, and the library plans to expand this part of the collection.

Although the library staff is used to dealing with requests that need immediate answers, the occasional question still arises that sends everyone into a scramble of research activity that can frustrate even the seasoned searcher. The answer to the "Jeopardy!" research staff inquiry: yes, okapis do use their prehensile tongues to clean their ears.

STATISTICS

Name of Zoo	Zoological Society of San Diego
	San Diego, California
Date Founded	1916
Name of Library	Zoological Society of San Diego Library
Telephone	619/231-1515
Name of Library Director	Michaele M. Robinson
	Manager of Library Services

Library Collection Size
  Number of Monographs   10,000
  Number of Subscriptions   600
  Main Subjects Collected   Vertebrate zoology, zoogeography, animal husbandry, animal behavior wildlife conservation, ecology
Staff size   1 Professional
                                          1 Paraprofessional
Online searching done   Yes
Interlibrary loans made   Yes
Network affiliations   OCLC

REFERENCE

Wegeforth, Harry M.; Morgan, Neil. *It began with a roar: the story of San Diego's world-famed zoo*. San Diego: Zoological Society of San Diego; 1969: Chapter 11.

Minnesota Zoological Garden Library

Angela Norell

SUMMARY. The Minnesota Zoological Garden is a relatively new zoo and maintains a professional library to support its goals of conservation and education. Computer-based activities are part of the management of current information services.

> In the end, we will conserve only what we love, we will love only what we understand, we will understand only what we are taught.
>
> *Baba Dioum*

HISTORY AND DESCRIPTION

This quotation reflects much of the philosophy of the establishment of the Minnesota Zoo which opened in 1978, making it one of the newest and largest zoos in the world. It has had the advantage of building on the experiences of other zoos in developing a facility using the latest technologies of animal exhibition and management. The zoo has specialized in Southeast Asian, Holarctic (Northern latitudes) and Minnesota wildlife, and marine mammals, exhibiting animals within natural environments. Its founders recognized the importance of research to support their goals of conservation and education along with the recreational aspects of a zoo, and established a library before the zoo opened. The librarian was originally a full-time professional position and is presently part-time. The li-

---

Angela Norell is Library/Information Resource Services Specialist, Minnesota Zoological Garden, St. Paul, MN 55124. She has an MLS degree from the University of Maryland.

© 1988 by The Haworth Press, Inc. All rights reserved.

brary has shared access to a staff secretary, volunteer assistants, and a computer.

The library is housed in the main zoo complex in what was originally a small gift shop, with one entire wall of windows facing a plaza. There are two departmental collections in buildings which are a mile away from the main complex: a medical collection in animal health, and horticulture.

This is the fourth location for the library since its inception 9 years ago. It was originally in the animal health building and then moved to the education/exhibit wing directly next to a live animal "touch and feel" room known as Zoolab. One of the librarian's original responsibilities was to substitute in Zoolab, and to handle several large snakes! When Zoolab expanded, the library was moved to a windowless room along a back hallway that had been used for animal equipment and food storage. When the card catalog, desk and boxes began to be moved in, one could expect to come in after being away for two days and find an empty cage placed atop the card catalog, straw bales on the floor, and distinctive smells in the air! Later, the space was officially converted into an office. The library was finally moved to its present location, which is more accessible to the major portion of the curatorial staff.

COLLECTION

The main subject areas are zoology, captive wildlife management, conservation, veterinary science, horticulture, marine mammals, aquatic science and natural history, with emphasis on the animals in the zoo's collection. With the necessity to successfully breed wild animals (purchasing a female clouded leopard may cost $10,000), and to maintain genetic diversity, there is a particular demand for information on reproduction and genetics. The library collection consists of approximately 3000 volumes including some rare books, and uses Library of Congress classification. In 1986, an animal index to 14 years of the annual and regional proceedings of the AAZPA (American Association of Zoological Parks and Aquariums) was prepared using a word processor, and distributed nationally, the first time such an index had been developed. Most of the papers on animals are arranged in files by ISIS number, which categorizes taxonomic schedules into a sixteen-digit numerical code.[1] The complete code is specific to subspecies, but for files, a seven-digit truncation to the family level is used. ISIS number files accommodate papers on related animals, and facilitate rapid coding. For example, a paper on the red panda is given the number 14 for the class Mammals, 12 for the order Carnivora, and 003 for the family Procyonidae. It is then filed alphabetically by common name within the family file Procyonidae.

Material selection is done cooperatively with suggestions from staff, recommendations of an ad hoc book selection committee representing various categories of staff, and from formal selection lists prepared by the librarian and submitted for staff review. The library currently operates with its own budget, although this coexists and sometimes fluctuates with departmental allocations for materials. Books purchased from departmental budgets must be reviewed by the librarian and are recorded and cataloged centrally. Cataloging is obtained primarily from a commercial vendor or done in-house. Materials are circulated without a formal due-date; items when borrowed are entered on the SCIMATE DBMS for retrieval by borrower, date loaned, or title.[2] This is particularly useful for checking a borrower's record at employment termination. Eventually this database will reflect the nonused materials in the library and can be used for weeding purposes. A paper bookcard file is also kept since the library is often "self-service."

SERVICES

The primary activities of the library revolve around current literature as found in *Current Contents: Agriculture, Biology and Environmental Sciences*, journals, and books. Many articles are obtained directly from authors around the world as referenced in *Current Contents* as well as through interlibrary loans. An in-house database using SCIMATE and an IBM-compatible computer with a hard-disk drive has been developed to manage these papers. Papers are coded using ten basic fields: author, title, source, year, ISIS number, genus species, common name, numerical subject codes, keywords and notes. Subject categories were developed using a variety of references including *Wildlife Review, Zoological Record*, and *BIOSIS*. The categories are arranged in a semi-hierarchical system and are assigned numerical codes with a keyword index so that a paper on parent-young interaction and care, for example, could be represented in the subject field simply by the number, 0220 Reproductive behavior. Files are arranged by broad taxonomic categories and loaded onto disks that can be given to supervisors for their personal DBMS. Data can be entered off-site by volunteers on compatible computers and merged into appropriate files.

Literature searches are done through *Wildlife Review*, an index covering more than 300 international journals on all aspects of wildlife management, databases such as BIOSIS, *Zoological Record* and MEDLINE. The zoo is part of the MINITEX network, and has access to academic collections in a four-state area, and the OCLC database. Interlibrary loans are also sent to libraries nationally. Networking unofficially with related libraries is essential. Zoo libraries are an invaluable resource and visits to other cities are never complete without contacting the resident zoo librarian! Other zoologically oriented institutions such as marine mammal organizations, veterinary science colleges, aquariums and other specialised agencies are valuable links to finding information. These linkages are established through directories, professional associations of the librarian and other staff members. The Research Centers Directory and the Conservation Directory which lists governmental and citizen groups involved with wildlife issues throughout the US and Canada are useful guides, along with directories published by special libraries such as the Directory of Aquarium Libraries. *Library News for Zoos and Aquariums*,[3] a tri-yearly newsletter, and the Union List of Journal Titles in AAZPA Libraries, are valuable sources of information and connection among the fifty-plus zoo libraries scattered throughout the world.

USERS

The library serves MZG staff, with additional access by special arrangement for student interns, researchers, volunteers, and other libraries. The staff includes curators, keepers, veterinary technicians, naturalists, horticulturists, administrators, researchers and graphic artists. Specialized users include the staff of ISIS, the International Species Inventory System, a computer-based information data bank collecting census and vital statistics on animals held in captivity. It identifies specific animals at individual zoos, establishes genetic lines of descent, projects future population growth among captive species around the world, provides breeding recommendations, and collects medical data for more than 100,000 animals. Also using the library is the AAZPA conservation coordinator, who manages species survival plans for long-term propagation of vanishing wild animals and is responsible to zoos internationally. These two offices have their own highly specialized book collections. There is a great deal of competition for positions; most of the supervisory staff have advanced degrees, and bachelor's degrees are common at the zookeeper level and many entry level positions.

The library was originally under the auspices of the Public Programs division, which consisted of the Marketing, Public Information, Education and Graphics and carried a full-time librarian position. In 1983 the position was reduced to half-time, and transferred to the Biological Programs Division which encompassed Animal Management, Animal Health, Horticulture, Exhibits, & Graphics and Research. There have been some positive results of this readjustment. The library reports directly to the Director for Biological Programs, whose responsibilities include research and conservation. In addition, the librarian works part-time at a major public library which is a great complement to the position at the zoo as it provides access to other librarians, professional journals, training programs, an unusually good collection of natural history and a large reference collection. Being the only librarian in a geographically isolated facility such as the zoo, these professional contacts and resources are very beneficial.

Volunteers are an important source of assistance ranging from clerical tasks performed regularly by several volunteers to special projects such as the animal index, for which all data entry was done by a single volunteer. The librarian maintains communication with volunteers who work in the library on days when she is absent with notes, phone calls, messages via the staff secretary, or by arranging personal meetings.

Working in a wildlife conservation institution such as the Minnesota Zoo with talented and committed professionals in their efforts to preserve increasingly rare animals and their disappearing ecosystems is a privilege and a challenge.

STATISTICS

Name of Zoo	Minnesota Zoological Garden
Date Founded	1978
Name of Library	Minnesota Zoological Garden Library
Name of Library Director	Angela Norell, Library/Information Resource Services Specialist
Telephone	612/431-9230
Library Collection Size	
Number of Monographs	3,000
Number of Subscriptions	70
Main Subjects Collected	Zoology, wildlife management, conservation, veterinary science, aquatic science, natural history.
Staff size	1 Part-time Professional
Online searching done	Yes
Interlibrary loans made	Yes
Network affiliations	MINITEX

REFERENCES

1. Flesness, N. R.; Garnatz, P. G.; Seal, U. S. ASIA—an Internation Specimen Information System. *In: Databases in systematics*. Edited by R. Allkin and F. A. Bisby. New York: Academic Press; 1984. (The Systematics Association Special Volume no. 26).
2. Wachtel, Ruth. Personal bibliographic databases. *Science*. 235: 1093-1096; 1987.
3. *Library News for Zoos and Aquariums*. Edited by Kay Kenyon, National Zoological Park Library, Washington, DC.

Cincinnati Zoo Library

Beatrice Orendorff

SUMMARY. This paper describes the facilities, collections and services of the Cincinnati Zoo Media Center Library. Plans for the future include expansion of its already extensive slide collection.

Where but in a Zoo Library could you find various animal skulls and other animal bones, whole animal skeletons, birds' nests and feathers and U.S. government confiscated animal skins being put to use in educational programs? The Cincinnati Zoo Media Center Library has all of the above and more!

FACILITIES AND COLLECTIONS

This Library was established in 1969 as a service to the zoo employees, volunteers and Zoo members. It is housed on the ground floor of the Education Department and contains approximately 2,700 books, 35 nature related periodicals and 15,000 slides. The Media Center is also home to a small number of film strips and records. All Zoo publications, such as docent newsletters, newspaper clippings of articles concerning the Zoo, and Zookeeper newsletters are collected. Complete collections of National Geographic magazines since 1934, National and International Wildlife Federation magazines since 1964 and Audubon Society magazines since 1980, are also housed here.

Until 2 years ago it was staffed by volunteers. In 1986 the Zoo hired a volunteer who had been a Tour Guide as well as a ZVI (Zoo volunteer interpreter) and office helper for 5 years, to staff the Me-

---

Beatrice Orendorff is Library Coordinator, Cincinnati Zoo Library, 3400 Vine St., Cincinnati, OH 45520.

© 1988 by The Haworth Press, Inc. All rights reserved.

dia Center on a full-time basis. It was felt that having a person present at all times would minimize the loss of books, which was great, and the loss of slides, which was enormous.

The book collection has since then been enlarged by approximately 300 titles, most of them Reference books. The new coordinator also started collecting local publications, such as Park news, Audubon Society news, Bird club news and Zoo Research Society news.

The slide collection has been enlarged and now contains 4,000 master slides which are housed in three professional slide cabinets. Three other cabinets house the 11,000 duplicate slides. These dupes are available through a check-out system to all Zoo employees as well as volunteers and can also be purchased. We now have sets of slides of Ohio mammals, birds, reptiles, fish and trees. Slide sets of animal feet are also available. Individuals as well as other Zoos and educational institutions are among those who have used the slides.

Our Zoo became a botanical garden in the summer of '87, which has generated a lot of interest in the Horticultural side of this institution, which, in turn, has created a demand for Horticulture slides. This need has been addressed by creating a new file for these slides.

SERVICES

Some of the services provided include the ordering of books for Zoo personnel and furnishing the Zoo's gift shop with a monthly list of recommended books for sale to Zoo visitors.

Providing a continuum to the Media Center has encouraged individuals to donate books, slides and magazine subscriptions to the Library. Through a careful system for checking out all material, losses have been kept to a bare minimum.

Plans for the future include a nature video library available for use by Zoo employees and volunteers, expansion of the book collection by 1,000 titles and expansion of the slide collection to include as many animal slides in all classes as possible. We are also working on slide sets of eyes, faces and animal coverings such as feathers, furs, scales etc. for use in programs on adaptation. We hope to include a great deal of very close views in these sets. All slides which have been published in our Guidebook, calendars and various pamphlets have been duplicated and are available for purchase or loan.

STATISTICS

Name of Zoo	Cincinnati Zoo and Botanical Garden
Date Founded	1875
Name of Library	Cincinnati Zoo Library
Telephone	513/281-3700
Name of Library Director	Beatrice Orendorff, Library Coordinator
Library Collection Size	
Number of Monographs	3,000
Number of Subscriptions	35
Main Subjects Collected	Zoology, wildlife conservation, animal physiology and anatomy, biology, animal and plant field guides, horticulture, ecology
Staff Size	1 Full-time employee
Online searching done	No
Interlibrary loans made	No
Network affiliations	None

American Zoological Park Libraries and Archives: Historical Considerations and Their Current Status

Vernon N. Kisling, Jr.

SUMMARY. Although accumulations of books have probably been a part of American zoological parks for as long as the zoological parks have been established, these accumulations have not been considered libraries until quite recently; most of these accumulations have only been established as libraries since the 1960s. Consideration is given to this historical development, followed by an analysis of the current (1987) status of these libraries. Specific information is presented on 78 libraries concerning their staffing, facilities, budgets, collection management, and services. Information is also presented on 32 archive collections.

AN HISTORICAL PERSPECTIVE

The zoological park, as distinct from the menagerie, began in America with the opening of the Philadelphia Zoological Park in 1874, it having been established by charter of the Philadelphia Zoological Society in 1859. By the turn of the century, some 16 zoological parks had become established, and today there are about 150.[1]

Although accumulations of books have, no doubt, been sitting on

---

Vernon N. Kisling, Jr. is Visiting Assistant University Librarian, Central Science Library, University of Florida, Gainesville, FL 32611. He has received the following degrees: DPA, Administration, Nova University; MS, Wildlife Biology, University of Georgia; MLS (exp), Library Science, Florida State University; BA, Zoology, University of South Florida.

The author would like to acknowledge his gratitude to all of those library staff members who took the time to provide information on their libraries.

© 1988 by The Haworth Press, Inc. All rights reserved.

the shelves of zoological park offices since their establishment, or soon afterwards, many of these accumulations have not been organized, or recognized, as libraries until quite recently. Most of these libraries have only been established since the 1960s, and even today in the 1980s very few of them have full-time librarians in charge of the collections.

Historically, the public zoological park grew out of the private menagerie, and the early management of the animals was a practical matter. Much of the required skills and information was passed on by word of mouth from keeper to keeper. In addition, early exhibits, diets, and general care did not require extensive knowledge from the literature.

However, as exhibit designs began to emphasize natural habitats, as diets began to imitate diets in the wild, as standards of general and veterinary care improved, and as captive propagation, conservation, and education programs became increasingly more sophisticated and important, the need for knowledge developed to the point that it could no longer be supplied by word of mouth or provided by a few individuals on the staff.

These matters received particularly serious attention during the 1960s, and the need for more information brought about a need for more publications and for the establishment of libraries. This growing body of knowledge and literature, and the increase in the number of libraries, has been a part of the continuing professionalization within the zoological park community. Guidelines are now available for establishing a zoological park library,[2] as is a core list of publications for starting the collection.[3] In addition, the AAZPA Librarians Special Interest Group maintains and distributes pertinent bibliographies as a service to AAZPA (American Association of Zoological Parks and Aquariums) members, and will provide assistance to zoological parks concerning library matters.[4]

CONTEMPORARY COLLECTIONS, MANAGEMENT, AND SERVICES

To determine the status of the zoological park libraries at this point in their development, a survey was conducted by the author in the fall of 1987. Previous surveys have not been as comprehensive;

however, one of these surveys (made in 1981) indicated that there were 104 zoological parks with libraries.[5,6,7] The survey by Kenyon (made in 1984) presented the view that out of these, only 40 should actually be considered libraries, based on the criteria that there should be someone with library skills in charge of the collection and that information services should be provided. Based on similar criteria, the survey by the author indicates that there could be 48 (those with full- or part-time librarians), or 63 (those providing circulation of the publications), or 53 (those providing reference, information, and/or interlibrary loan services) libraries. However, of these only 11 have full-time librarians to provide collection management and assistance, circulation of the publications, and some kind of information service. (Refer to the section on Library Services for information on the number of libraries providing various combinations of these services.)

This survey was sent to 117 U.S. zoological parks and aquariums, including all of those accredited by the AAZPA as of September 1986.[8] AAZPA accreditation standards do not require a zoological park to maintain a library and do not define what a library should be; however, the zoological park staff is expected to have access to reference materials. These may be located at the zoological park or at a nearby library to which the staff has access.[9] No attempt was made in this study to define what constitutes a library or to define the term librarian. As has been pointed out, determining the number of zoological park libraries really depends on the mix of criteria one chooses to define what constitutes a library, and that has not been done here.

•*General Information*

- 117 Total number of zoological parks surveyed.
- 80 Zoological parks responding to the survey (68%).
- 78 Zoological parks with libraries. These are the libraries upon which the remaining information is based. It should be noted though that out of the 37 zoological parks not responding to the survey the author has personal knowledge of 11 that have staff responsible for the collections and that may also be considered libraries.

Establishment of the Libraries

Although some 16 zoological parks existed prior to 1900, only one claims to have established a library prior to this year. The first library was established at the National Zoological Park in 1898. This was followed by libraries at the New York Zoological Park in 1900, the San Diego Zoological Park in 1916, the Cheyenne Mountain Zoological Park in 1927, the San Antonio Zoological Gardens in 1929, the Toledo Zoological Park in 1937, and the Mesker Park Zoo in 1945. Four others were established during the 1950s, and all of the others were established during and since the 1960s.

It should be noted that of the 37 zoological parks not responding to the survey, and of the 12 that responded but did not provide the date of their establishment, several were founded prior to the 1960s and could possibly have established their libraries prior to this time. Some of those responding to the survey had to estimate the date of establishment, there being no formal or well documented transformation of their book accumulations into libraries.

•*Date of Establishment*

- 12 Libraries with no date or an unknown date of establishment.
- 1 Library established prior to 1900.
- 6 Libraries established 1900-1949.
- 4 Libraries established 1950-1959.
- 14 Libraries established 1960-1969.
- 23 Libraries established 1970-1979.
- 18 Libraries established 1980-1987.

•*Origins of the Original Publications*

- 15 Original publications are of unknown origins.
- 19 Original publications in the collection were donated (usually from an early zoo director, staff member, or benefactor).
- 23 Original publications in the collection were donated and/or purchased.
- 21 Original publications in the collection were purchased.

Library Staffing

Zoological park libraries vary greatly in their physical size and in the services provided. The emphasis put on them by their zoological park administrators varies as well. Thus, the staffing of the libraries varies considerably. Most library staff members are also education curators, administrative secretaries, or volunteers from the zoological park staff or from the zoological society. There are few full-time positions with the library as their sole responsibility, and few with the position title of "Librarian" or its equivalent.

•*Librarians-General*

- 18 Full-time librarians. Of these, 8 are titled "Librarian," 4 are education curators, 2 are secretaries, and 4 provided no titles.
- 30 Part-time librarians, of these; 6 are titled "Librarians" (or Resource Specialist, Manager—Library Services, etc.).

•*Librarians-Academic Backgrounds*

- 18 Librarians having a BA/BS degree.
- 4 Librarians having an MA/MS degree.
- 9 Librarians having an MLS degree.
- 2 Librarians having a PhD degree.

•*Librarians-Number of Library Staff Members*

- 25 Libraries with no zoo staff members assigned to the library.
- 38 Libraries with 1 library staff member.
- 7 Libraries with 2 library staff members.
- 3 Libraries with 3 library staff members.
- 5 Libraries with multiple volunteers. Several of the above libraries also use volunteers, but they are in addition to the staff members.

Library Facilities, Collections, and Budgets

The size of zoological park libraries range from a few shelves to over 2,000 square feet, a handful of books to 12,000 volumes, a few journals to 1,000 subscriptions, a few newsletters to over 200 subscriptions or exchanges, and budgets ranging from none (or variable) to $90,000.

- **Size of the Facility**

    22 Unknown or unspecified square footage.
    44 Library area 1-500 square feet in size.
     7 Library area 501-1,000 square feet in size.
     4 Library area 1,001-2,000 square feet in size (John G. Shedd Aquarium, Lee Richardson Zoological Park, San Diego Zoological Park, and Toledo Zoological Park).
     1 Library area 2,345 square feet in size (New York Zoological Park).

- **Location of the Library**

     3 Library is a separate entity (however, not a separate building).
    43 Library is located in the administration building.
     3 Library is located in the administration-education building.
    22 Library is located in the education building or office.
     3 Library is located in another zoological park building.
     4 Library is in multiple locations.

- **Number of Books**

     6 Unknown or unspecified number of books.
    26 Libraries with 1-500 books in their collection.
    22 Libraries with 501-1,000 books in their collection.
    14 Libraries with 1,001-2,000 books in their collection.
     4 Libraries with 2,001-3,000 books in their collection.
     2 Libraries with 3,001-4,000 books in their collection.
     1 Library with 5,500 books (Chicago Zoological Park).
     1 Library with 6,000 books (New York Zoological Park).
     1 Library with 7,500 books (John G. Shedd Aquarium).
     1 Library with 12,000 books (San Diego Zoological Park).

•Number of Journals

20 Unknown or unspecified number of journal subscriptions.
35 Libraries with 1-25 journal subscriptions.
8 Libraries with 26-50 journal subscriptions.
6 Libraries with 51-100 journal subscriptions.
4 Libraries with 101-200 journal subscriptions.
2 Libraries with 201-300 journal subscriptions.
1 Library with 350 journals (National Zoological Park).
1 Library with 605 journals (San Diego Zoological Park).
1 Library with 1,000 journals (Discovery Island, Disney World).

•Number of Newsletters

38 Unknown or unspecified number of newsletter subscriptions or exchanges (many zoological parks exchange subscriptions with each other).
27 Libraries with 1-50 newsletters.
7 Libraries with 51-100 newsletters.
5 Libraries with 101-200 newsletters.
1 Library with 200+ newsletters (Lincoln Park Zoo).

•Other Library Materials

44 Libraries with slides and/or photographs.
32 Libraries with reprints.
14 Libraries with maps.
6 Libraries with videotapes.
5 Libraries with microforms.
8 Libraries with other material: vertical files (2), annual reports (2), and species files, zoo guides, posters & post cards, artifacts (1 each).

•Classification of the Publications

25 Libraries using Library of Congress class numbers.
18 Libraries using Dewey Decimal class numbers.
8 Libraries using another system — scheme by subject.
16 Libraries using another system — scheme not stated.
11 Libraries using no classification scheme.

•Library Budgets

- 32 Unknown or unspecified budgets. Many do not have budgets specifically for the library or it fluctuates from year to year. Information was requested on the amount spent annually for publications, however, the higher figures provided below may be budgets for the entire operation of the libraries.
- 10 Libraries with $1-$500 budgets.
- 14 Libraries with $501-$1,000 budgets.
- 6 Libraries with $1,001-$2,000 budgets.
- 1 Library with $2,001-$3,000 budget.
- 6 Libraries with $4,000-$5,000 budgets.
- 2 Libraries with $5,001-$7,000 budgets.
- 5 Libraries with $10,000-$30,000 budgets.
- 1 Library with $37,000 budget (San Diego Zoological Park).
- 1 Library with $90,000 budget (Chicago Zoological Park).

•Subjects Collected

Subjects listed as receiving emphasis include: vertebrate zoology (35), wildlife ecology/natural history (25), captive management (17), wildlife conservation (11), veterinary medicine (11), botany/horticulture (10), animal behavior (9), marine biology/oceanography (6), native/regional wildlife (4), nutrition (2), education/research (2), species identification (1), zoo history (1), tropical biology (1), photography (1), and children's books (1).

Library Services

As has been noted, providing services is one of the criteria that has been recommended for use in defining a library. While quite a few of the libraries provide some kind of information service, the number of libraries providing a combination of two or more of these services is less, but varies depending on the combination of services. These services are always provided to the zoological park staff; however, they are not always provided to the outside community. Thus, the zoological park library as a community information resource is limited. So is the use of computers at these libraries, with only 22 of them using computers, and only 6 of these being connected to a computer network. Thus, access to information is also limited.

•Services of the Libraries

- 15 Libraries providing interlibrary loan service. Some of these libraries have restrictions: to zoo libraries only (2), per page charges (2), ALA forms required (1), and photocopies only (1).
- 53 Libraries providing reference service.
- 6 Libraries providing general information (without providing what would be considered reference service).
- 32 Libraries providing photocopying service.
- 63 Libraries providing circulation of the publications. Some of these libraries have restrictions: zoo staff only (27), staff & volunteers only (26), and staff & zoo society members (1).

•Combinations of These Library Services

- 20 Reference/general information and circulation.
- 15 Reference/general information, photocopying, and circulation.
- 13 Circulation only.
- 12 Reference/general information, photocopying, circulation, and interlibrary loan (ALL of the services).
- 6 Reference/general information only.
- 4 Reference/general information and photocopying.
- 4 NONE of these services.
- 2 Reference/general information, photocopying, and interlibrary loan.
- 1 Circulation and interlibrary loan.
- 1 Photocopying only.

•Full Service Libraries

- 11 Libraries with a full-time librarian, circulation services, and information services (reference, general information, photocopying, and/or interlibrary loan): Chicago Zoological Park, Indianapolis Zoological Park, John G. Shedd Aquarium, Lee Richardson Zoological Park, National

Aquarium at Baltimore, National Zoological Park, New York Zoological Park, Northwest Trek Wildlife Park, San Diego Zoological Park, Santa Fe Community College Teaching Zoo, and Tulsa Zoological Park.

•*Patrons Served by the Libraries*

78 Zoo administrators and curators.
78 Keeper staff (this category also often includes volunteers).
47 Zoological society members (sometimes this category only includes the docents).
6 Zoological society members by appointment.
42 Outside researchers.
4 Outside researchers by appointment.
30 Local schools.
6 Local schools by appointment.
7 General public.
36 General public by appointment.

•*Computer Use in the Libraries*

22 Libraries using computers. Uses include: use in place of the card catalog (3), use along with the card catalog (8), online research (9), networking (OCLC 4) (SCIMATE/DBMS 1) (LUIS cataloging system 1), word processing (7), cataloging or printing catalog cards (6), circulation records (3), book purchasing (3), publication inventory (3), animal records (2), ARKS animal record system (1), labels (1), bookkeeping (1), fund raising (1), studbooks (1), and electronic mail (1).

THE ARCHIVE COLLECTIONS

Of the libraries responding to the survey, 32 (41%) have archive collections; however, out of these only 11 are cataloged. No doubt many more zoological parks have archival material, but this material is probably scattered throughout the files and offices of the zoological park, the zoological society, and the municipal agencies responsible for the zoological park.

In only two cases was it stated that this archival material was being studied. With the centennial anniversary of the first American zoological park now past, and with several more coming in the near future, it would be useful for these archival materials to be organized, cataloged, and restored so that they may be studied. At the present time it is very difficult to study the history of an individual zoological park or the overall history of American zoological parks. It is hoped that with the increasing number of centennial celebrations occurring in the near future, the zoological parks will be encouraged to properly maintain their historical records and that they will include archival collections within their libraries.

•*Archive Collections*

32 Zoological parks with archives.
4   Archives cared for by an archivist.
14 Archives cared for by a librarian.
14 Archives cared for by someone else: staff member (4), volunteers (2), private individual (1), and unstated (7).
11 Archive collections that are cataloged.
5   Archive collections that are being restored.
2   Archive collections that are being studied.
22 Libraries/archives containing rare books (pre-1900).
6   Libraries/archives actively collecting rare books (pre-1900).

•*Materials Collected*

Archive material specifically named as being included in the collections: institutional records (23), photographs (9), newspaper clippings (8), memorabilia/promotional material (3), oral history tapes (2), exhibit plans (1), old veterinary tools (1), and old photographic equipment (1).

REFERENCE NOTES

1. The actual number of zoological parks (and aquariums) varies. The official directory of the American Association of Zoological Parks & Aquariums (AAZPA), *Zoological Parks and Aquariums in the Americas 1984-85* (Boyd, Linda J. [ed]. Wheeling, WV: AAZPA; 1984) lists 158 (the newer edition of this directory lists only the accredited zoos). The *International Zoo Yearbook* (P.J.S. Olney [ed]. London: Zoological Society of London; 1986: Volume 24/25, pp.

347-414) lists 152. *The Official Museum Directory* (The American Association of Museums. Wilmette IL: National Register Publishing; 1986) lists 147.

2. Kenyon, Kay. *Suggested guidelines for zoo and aquarium libraries*. Washington: AAZPA Librarians Special Interest Group and National Zoological Park Library; 1986.

3. Kenyon, Kay. *A recommended list of books and other information resources for zoo and aquarium libraries*. Washington: National Zoological Park Library; 1987.

4. AAZPA Librarians Special Interest Group, Attn: Kay Kenyon, Chair, National Zoological Park Library, Washington DC 20008.

5. Miller, Gail D. An inquiry into the role of libraries in zoos and aquariums. (M.S. Thesis). University of Chicago; 1981.

6. Kenyon, Kay. Zoo/aquarium libraries, a survey. *Special Libraries*. 75 (4): 329-334; 1984 October.

7. Finlay, Ted W.; Maple, Terry L. A survey of research in American zoos and aquariums. *Zoo Biology*. 5 (3): 261-268; 1986.

8. Anon. AAZPA recognizes accredited institutions. *AAZPA Newsletter*. 27(11): 21; 1986 November.

9. Anon. *Accreditation of zoos and aquariums*. Wheeling, WV: American Association of Zoological Parks and Aquariums; 1987. Wagner, Robert O. [Letter to Vernon Kisling]; 1987 October 2.

SCI-TECH COLLECTIONS

Tony Stankus, Editor

This issue's column on Superconductivity has had an interesting history. It started out as a class project in a course entitled "Library materials and Information Services in Science and Technology" at the University of Rhode Island. On hearing of it, I asked for a copy and was treated to three editions as events, including the announcement of the Nobel Prize in Physics for Superconductivity in 1987, forced revisions. I feel that the final product will be useful for some time to come, particularly for its outline of the historical development of the field. I am also glad to aid in the professional development of the two new librarian coauthors. I think that the library and information science communities have a lesson to learn from law school reviews. In those publications, faculty oversee the rather exhaustive survey papers of law students. Not only are the articles useful educational exercises for the student's own training, they are highly cited in legal briefs in actual cases. Can we learn from the energetic efforts of our students? I invite further submissions from this pool of talent.

Superconductivity: A Brief Guide to the Research and Literature

C. Herbert Carson
James A. Barrett
Mary Jean Colburn

SUMMARY. This article helps the reader gain an understanding of superconductivity. It presents a brief history, identifies principal researchers and their institutions, discusses its importance in the world marketplace, and provides a list of resources for obtaining further information. A glossary of terms is also included.

INTRODUCTION

Superconductivity is a property discovered in an increasing number of electrically conducting solids in which their resistance to the flow of electrons vanishes.[1] Until recently superconductivity was detected in only a few materials, and most critically, only at temperatures near absolute zero (-459 F.), a combination of circumstances that made the discovery seem industrially impractical. Funding for this research had actually dropped for much of the century because progress was so slow. It was thought of as a "rust

---

C. Herbert Carson is an instructor, and James A. Barrett and Mary Jean Colburn are graduate students in the MLIS program at the Graduate School of Library and Information Studies at the University of Rhode Island, Kingston, RI, 02881-0815. Carson holds a PhD from Syracuse University, Barrett has a BA from Suffolk University, and Colburn holds a BA from the University of New Hampshire.

Appreciation is extended to Candice A. Freeman for providing research assistance for this paper.

© 1988 by The Haworth Press, Inc. All rights reserved.

belt" area of research.[2] See Figure 1 for an illustration of the primary milestones in the history of superconductivity.

Superconductivity was first observed in 1911 in Leyden, the Netherlands, by H. Kammerlingh Onnes. He was able to reduce mercury to a superconducting state of 4.2 degrees above absolute zero.[3] While he was awarded the Nobel Prize for this discovery in 1915, neither he nor others could fully explain the phenomenon for a number of decades.

In 1933, Walther Meissner and R. Ochsenfeld observed that a metal cooled into the superconducting state could actually expel its own magnetic field in a number of instances. This Meissner Effect was an important discovery because it indicated that superconduc-

```
                            Figure 1

      - Now -------------- Reports of superconductivity at
                           -28°F (240°K)

      - February, 1987 --  Houston team led by Paul Chu
                           reaches -284°F (98°K)

      - 1986 ------------- Superconducting oxides discovered
                           by Muller and Bednorz at -406°F
                           (35°K)


      - 1973 ------------- Niobium alloy raised to -419°F
                           (23°K)
Y
E
A
R

      -1941 -------------- Discovery of niobium alloy that is
                           superconductive at -433°F (15°K)




      -1911 -------------- Superconductivity is discovered at
                           -452°F (4°K)
```

tivity was a quantum-mechanical phenomenon. This fortuitously revived interest in the field since quantum mechanics was becoming quite a well-supported area at that time.[4]

A small number of discoveries was again noted in the 1950s. It was shown that the flow of electrons in some solids was hindered by the vibrations of the atoms that make up that solid. It was this hindrance that caused resistance and required the compensating force we call voltage to overcome that resistance. It was suggested that the "freezing" of vibrations at traditional superconducting temperatures actually reduced energy-wasting collisions of electrons. A specific mechanism was suggested in 1957 by Bardeen, Cooper, and Schrieffer. They postulated that in superconductivity, normally chaotic, colliding electrons nicely pair off, accounting for the disappearance of the chaos and the resistance.[5] Interest in this explanation sharply increased when Josephson showed that these orderly Cooper pairs can tunnel through insulating barriers between superconductors.[6] Since the controllable tunneling of electrons through solids is the underlying principle of computer circuitry, the promise of incredibly smoother flow using superconducting solids revived failing financial support at that time. Bardeen, Cooper, and Schrieffer were eventually to win a Nobel Prize in 1972 for the success of their theory. But its practical application still had a seemingly unshakable requirement for industrially impractical near-absolute-zero-environments.

The breakthrough would come almost 15 years later. Karl Alex Muller and Johannes Georg Bednorz observed that the critical temperature could be raised 12 degrees with some materials. The point was not that the temperature modification was large, it was that it occurred at all. They published their findings in the respectable, but not characteristically trend-setting West German journal, *Zeitschrift für Physik*, at first eliciting little response. But by December 4, 1986, researchers from Tokyo and Houston had announced confirmation of the findings at the annual meeting of the Materials Research Society. The situation was like the four minute mile: once the barrier was down, it seemed as if everyone could break it. Research groups began frantically searching for new superconducting materials in the renewed hope that it might be possible to achieve superconductivity at near room temperatures, and win a Nobel Prize.

The American start seemed suspicious. In February 1987, Chu of Houston and Wu of Alabama achieved superconductivity in a yttrium compound at 98K. Frank Press, president of the National Academy of Sciences said: "Superconductivity has become the test case of whether the U.S. has a technological future."[7] In July 1987, President Reagan announced a new Superconductivity Initiative Proposal, and the nation was committed.

The Japanese seemed determined to win in both the research lab and on the factory floor. The Japanese Ministry of International Trade and Industry (MITI) announced the formation of a consortium to coordinate an all out effort to exploit the new technology.[8] The April 1987 issue of the *Japanese Journal of Applied Physics* carried an astounding 84 articles on superconductivity.

It seemed ironic that neither an American nor Japanese group got the Nobel prize in October 1987. However, in light of the Nobel Committee's penchant for awarding people who have sustained an interest in superconductivity through its long and not always promising history, it was not entirely unpredictable that the stolid Europeans, Bednorz and Muller, would receive it. What is even more predictable is that research will continue feverishly and that more applications are being explored. For a representative sampling of who is conducting research and where it is being conducted see Figure 2.

CURRENT AND POTENTIAL APPLICATIONS

The application of superconductivity is important because of its potential to vastly improve performance. While theorists continue to puzzle over why the new superconductors work so well (most agree that the same mechanism is operating in all the new oxide superconductors) bench physicists, relying on dogged trial and error experimentation (the Edisonian approach), keep making them work better.[9] Tasks may soon be possible that only a short time ago were thought to be impractical. Superconductivity will affect every aspect of electricity and profoundly change the way we live if developments continue as rapidly in the near future.

Figure 2

Researcher	Institution
Philip W. Anderson	Princeton University
Bertram Batlogg	AT&T Bell Labs
Johannes G. Bednorz	IBM - Zurich
H. Kent Bowen	Massachusetts Institute of Technology
Robert Cava	AT&T Bell Labs
Paul C.W. Chu	University of Houston
Marvin Cohen	University of California, Berkeley
Frank Fradin	Argonne National Laboratory
Donald Ginsberg	University of Illinois
Laura Greene	Massachusetts Institute of Technology
John Hulm	Westinghouse
Alex B. Malozemoff	IBM
F.C. Moon	Cornell University
Karl Alex Muller	IBM - Zurich
Brian Schwartz	National Magnet Laboratory
Shoji Tanaka	University of Tokyo
Lowell Wegner	Wayne State
Maw-Kuen Wu	University of Alabama

The Japanese have been particularly interested in using superconductivity in magnetically levitated (maglev) trains, an interest they share with the French and the West Germans, but which Americans lost in the 1970s. The British are starting to organize but fear they'll never catch up.[10] Australia has an abundance of rare earths useful in making some superconductors, and is developing some research programs.[11]

As has been discussed, the Japanese are testing a high speed train that can compete with air travel. An earlier unmanned version set the speed record in 1979 at 321 miles per hour. These maglev trains run smoothly and in relative silence without the friction of wheel against rail.[12]

Computers would be dramatically improved and drastically reduced in size. Superconductors eliminate the friction which causes heat. Computers today are limited in the amount of chips they are able to have by the heat that the circuits generate. The development of superconductors would mean small computers could hold many more chips.[13]

Electricity would cost less. Twenty percent of the energy sent through conventional cables is lost through heat. Theoretically, if sent through a superconducting cable, *no* energy would be lost.[14]

Recent tests at the Ultrafast Science Center of the University of Rochester showed a device made at Cornell University that enables the new generation of superconductors to transmit data at speeds up to 100 times faster than today's state of the art optical fiber networks. Very short electrical pulses were measured in trillionths of a second with no distortion. This means that the entire contents of the Library of Congress could be transmitted in two minutes.[15]

Magnetic resonance imaging machines, which hospitals use to diagnose brain tumors, would become much cheaper and smaller. Today they have thousands of dollars worth of insulation to preserve the liquid helium coolant. Costs would be cut drastically by using the new generation of superconducting materials.

In a study done in 1978, NASA suggested other potential applications for superconductivity. They are (a) instruments for gravitational studies, some of which could be useful for navigation (gyroscopes, accelerometers, stable oscillators), and (b) fusion reactors or magnetohydrodynamic (MHD) generators for energy production, the mass-driver system, and plasma or MHD propulsion engines, etc.[16]

MONOGRAPHS

At the time this article was sent to press no monographs about high temperature superconductivity had yet been published. However, information about low temperature superconductivity can be obtained from the following sources: For a general introduction to superconductivity, McDonald provides a clear and authoritative guide in *Near Zero: the Physics of Low Temperature Physics*. Also, Lynton's *Superconductivity* provides a brief survey for readers with a basic knowledge of physics.

Separate monographs by Blatt, Rickayzen, and Schrieffer, discuss theories of superconductivity. Each work is entitled *Theory of Superconductivity*. Blatt's book surveys present theories and experiments, such as the Bose-Einstein gas model, the quasi-chemical equilibrium theory, and theories of Bogoliubov, Zubarev, and Tserkovnikov. Rickayzen traces the development of superconductivity theory in the twentieth century and provides a detailed discussion of macroscopic and microscopic theories. This book requires a beginning acquaintance with quantum mechanics. Schrieffer's book is an introduction to the more difficult concepts of superconductivity.

Newhouse discusses the application of theory to superconducting films, solenoids, amplifiers, switching devices, and storage devices in *Applied Superconductivity*. Practical devices for use especially in computer memories are analyzed in Bremer's *Superconductive Devices*. A physical understanding of superconductivity, especially type II superconductors, is provided in DeGennes' *Superconductivity in Metals and Alloys*.

Other monographs that deal with more specific aspects of superconductivity include Solymar's *Superconductive Tunneling and Applications*, Van Duzer and Turner's *Principles of Superconducting Devices and Circuits*, and *Superconductivity in Magnetic and Exotic Materials* from the Taniguichi International Symposium.

INDICES AND DATABASES

The most reliable indices in print format include *Physics Abstracts, Current Physics Index, Science Citation Index, Engineering Index, Electrical and Electronics Abstracts, Chemical Abstracts*, and *Technical Abstract Bulletin*. For citations of translations of non-English journal articles, see *Technical Translations*.

Various databases were examined to identify those that cite articles about superconductivity most often. A free text search was conducted using the truncated term "superconduct." Figure 3 is a list of the databases that contain the greatest number of postings. A search was also conducted to determine which journals were cited most often in 1986 and in 1987 through mid-November. Figure 4 lists those journals cited most often in INSPEC.

Both INSPEC and SCISEARCH shows increases in the number of articles about superconductivity in 1987, even though the 1987 search only covered about ten and one-half months of postings. These figures provide an indication of the increased interest in this area of research, but is probably not a true indication of the overall amount of research being conducted as a result of the new discoveries. The time lag that occurs from the time a research article is submitted for publication in a refereed journal to the time it is entered in the database prevents us from gaining an accurate perspective of the increase in research on superconductivity.

The fact that superconductivity articles are cited most often in *Solid State Communications* and *Physical Review Letters* indicates

Figure 3

DATABASE	TOTAL	SUPERCONDUCT POSTINGS 1986	1987
INSPEC (1977-Nov., 1987)	23255	1830	2075
SCISEARCH (1984-Nov., 1987)	4479	808	1622
COMPENDEX (1970-Nov., 1987)	14482	704	616
NTIS (1964-Nov., 1987)	8302	328	92

Figure 4

JOURNAL	SUPERCONDUCT POSTINGS 1986	1987
Solid State Communications	69	120
Physical Review Letters	56	64
Journal of Applied Physics	58	38
Cryogenics	38	35
Journal of Low Temperature Physics	48	30

the desire to publish results of research in the most expedient manner. Thus, it is necessary to be aware of the sources that provide the most up-to-date information.

The desire to exchange information expediently has also resulted in the appearance of several newsletters devoted solely to this topic. Following are brief descriptions of seven publications that were distributed at the Federal Conference on Commercial Applications of Superconductivity in July 1987. *High-Tc Update* is published twice a month by the Ames Laboratory of Iowa State University. "It contains brief descriptions of experiments, the compounds used and difficulties encountered, along with possible correctives."[17] *Inside Energy* is a 10-page weekly newsletter that covers energy concerns, including superconductivity. MIT's Materials Processing Center publishes a monthly report called, *Materials and Processing Report*. *New Technology Week,* which calls itself "the newspaper of superconductors/materials sciences/power electronics/high energy physics," is published by the King Communications Group, Inc. Business Publishers Inc. publishes a readable and newsy weekly newsletter called *Superconductivity*. *Superconductivity News* is a monthly newsletter aimed at examining applications of superconductivity, evaluating companies, and listing stock prices. Finally, *Superconductor Week* covers basic research work and emphasizes governmental actions.

These newsletters and the journals listed in Figure 4 are primarily for scientists and/or technologists. Numerous articles are also available for the layman to learn about superconductivity. See Appendix 3 for a brief list of articles that are recommended for a nontechnical overview of the topic.

NONPRINT RESOURCES

Today, information can often become available more readily using electronic media formats. Nonprint materials such as video should not be overlooked as resources for providing scientists and technologists with up-to-date information on superconductivity.

For example, the American Physical Society, host of a March 18, 1987, meeting attended by 2500 scientists is selling videotapes of the eight-hour session for up to $200. Also, the Materials Research

Society is selling a seven-hour videotape of its April 1987 meeting in Anaheim, California, for $165. Scientists from ten countries delivered papers at this meeting and discussed potential applications of the new materials.

CONCLUSIONS

Although there has been much optimism expressed regarding the future of superconductivity, there are numerous technical problems that must be overcome before application becomes reality. Alan Schriesheim, director of Argonne National Laboratory, says, "Where we stand now is like at the beginning of the transistor or the laser. We can't really foresee how we're going to work out the bugs or what these superconductors might be used for in the future."[18]

A theory that explains why these materials become superconducting must be found. Without the theory the Edisonian approach will continue to be the only method for finding better superconductors, consuming valuable time and resources.

The current limitations of the superconducting materials may restrict their use on a practical level. "The biggest obstacle so far has been that these materials cease to be superconducting as soon as researchers try to pass anything more than a very small current through them."[19] Until greater currents can be transmitted, most practical applications will not be possible.

In addition, the thin film technology used to coat wires with superconducting materials is extremely expensive. A better method is needed in order for practical application to be cost-effective.

Despite problems such as these, most scientists working in this area appear to be optimistic. The pace of new discoveries appears to have lessened, but the scientists and technologists will still need to obtain information about the most recent discoveries as soon as possible. This article provides a basic understanding of superconductivity for the information specialist by presenting an overview of research, both past and present. Potential applications of superconductors have been examined as well as sources used by the specialists. A basic list of resources and nontechnical articles have been provided for the nonspecialist.

REFERENCES

1. Parlere, Sybil P. (ed.). *McGraw-Hill dictionary of scientific and technical terms*. 3rd ed. New York: McGraw-Hill; 1984.
2. Muller, F.M. Breakthroughs in superconductivity. *Journal of Metals*. 39:6-8; 1987 May.
3. *McGraw-Hill encyclopedia of science and technology*. New York: McGraw-Hill; 1977.
4. Halsey, W.D. (ed.). *Colliers encyclopedia with bibliography and index*. New York: Macmillan Educational Co.; 1984.
5. Ibid.
6. McGraw-Hill, Op. Cit.
7. Russakoff, D. Superchallenge; two different cadences in the superconductor race; U.S. marshalling free-market forces. *Washington Post*. 110(166):A1; 1987 May 20.
8. Burgess, J. Superchallenge; two different cadences in the superconductor race; Japanese seeding a united front. *Washington Post*. 110(166):A16; 1987 May 20.
9. The new superconductivity. *Scientific American*. 256: 32; 1987 June.
10. Britain's superconductor teams compare notes and budgets. *Nature*. 327:4; 1987 May 7.
11. Australian scientists struggling to join the superconductor race. *Nature*. 327:649; 1987 June 25.
12. Sullivan, W. Race for the fastest train: Japan builds a new prototype. *New York Times*. 137(47,236):C1, C13; 1987 September 15.
13. Sullivan, D.B. (ed.). *The role of superconductivity in the space program: an assessment of present capabilities and future potential*. Boulder, Colorado: National Bureau of Standards; 1978.
14. Lemonick, M. Superconductors. *Time*. 129(19): 65; 1987 May 11.
15. Gleick, J. New frontiers of communication lie in test superconductor device. *New York Times*. 137(47,280):1+; 1987 October 2.
16. Sullivan, Op. Cit.
17. Covering superconductivity. *Physics Today*. 40(9): 54; 1987 September.
18. Maranto, Gina. Superconductivity: hype vs. reality. *Discover*. 8(8):32, 1987 August.
19. Bass, A. Superconductivity research: pace slows, reality catches up. *Boston Globe*. 232(134):53, 56; 1987 November 9.

APPENDIX 1: MONOGRAPHS DISCUSSED

Blatt, J.M. *Theory of superconductivity*. New York: Academic; 1964.
Bremer, J.W. *Superconductive devices*. New York: McGraw-Hill; 1962.
DeGennes, P.G. *Superconductivity in metals and alloys*. New York: W.A. Benjamin; 1966.

Lynton, E.A. *Superconductivity*. 3rd ed. London: Methuen; 1969.
MacDonald, D.K.C. *Near zero: the physics of low temperature physics*. London: Heinemann; 1963.
Newhouse, V.L. *Applied superconductivity*. New York: Wiley; 1964.
Rickayzen, G. *Theory of superconductivity*. New York: Wiley; 1965.
Schrieffer, J.R. *Theory of superconductivity*. New York: W.A. Benjamin; 1964.
Solymar, L. *Superconductive tunneling and applications*. New York: Wiley-Interscience; 1972.
Taniguichi International Symposium. *Superconductivity in magnetic and exotic materials*. Kashojima, Japan; 1983.
Van Duzer, T.; Turner, C. *Principles of superconducting devices and circuits*. New York: Elsevier North Holland; 1981.

APPENDIX 2: RECOMMENDED NON-TECHNICAL ARTICLES

Campbell, P. A superconductivity primer. *Nature*, 330: 21-24; 1987 November 5.
Lemonick, M.D. Superconductors. *Time*. 129:64-70+; 1987 May 11.
Maranto, G. Superconductivity: hype vs. reality. *Discover*. 8:22-24; 1987 August.
Fisher, A. Superconductor frenzy. *Popular Science*. 231: 34-38; 1987 July.
Wilson, J.W.; Port, O. Our life has changed. *Business Week*. 94-100; 1987 April 6.
Search and discover: superconductivity seen above the boiling point of nitrogen. *Physics Today*. 40(4): 17-23; 1987 April.

APPENDIX 3: GLOSSARY[1]

Absolute zero: The least possible temperature that could theoretically exist, according to the first and second laws of thermodynamics. At this temperature thermal energy is nil, but zero-point energy, attributed to the atoms by quantum mechanics, persists.
BCS theory: Postulates that superconductivity occurs when electrons become bound into pairs, called Cooper pairs. The theory does not specify how this pairing occurs.
Cooper pairs: Electrons that attract each other, no matter how weakly, will condense into a bound state. The attractive mechanism is called an electron-phonon interaction.
Josephson effect: An effect concerning the behavior of two superconductors separated by such a small gap that their wave functions overlap. Josephson predicted (correctly) that under certain conditions the frequencies and phases of the two sets of wave functions would be related and that there would be tunneling of electron

---

1. Definitions taken from: Thewlis, J. *Concise dictionary of physics*. Oxford: Pergamon; 1979.

pairs across the gap; and that there would be interactions between this tunnelling current and the magnetic and electric fields in which the junction was situated.

Magnetohydrodynamics (MHD): The study of electromagnetic phenomena in electrically conducting fluids. The fluid may be a molten metal or ionized gas (plasma).

Meissner effect: When a superconductor is cooled in a magnetic field from above the critical temperature to below that temperature the magnetic flux is expelled from the material with a sudden change in the field strength outside.

Superconductivity: The disappearance or near disappearance of the electrical resistance of certain metals, alloys, and compounds at temperatures below a transition temperature which is characteristic of the substance concerned and its known as the critical temperature (T_c) for that substance.

Superconductor: A substance exhibiting superconductivity. Two types of superconductor are recognized: type I superconductors, for which flux penetration occurs over a very narrow range of magnetic field; and type II superconductors, for which it occurs over a comparatively wide range.

NEW REFERENCE WORKS IN SCIENCE AND TECHNOLOGY

Robert G. Krupp, Editor

Reviewers for this column are: Carmela Carbone (CC), Engineering Societies Library, New York, NY; Kerry L. Kresse (KLK), University of Kentucky, KY; Robert G. Krupp (RGK), Maplewood, NJ; Donna Lee (DL), University of Vermont, Burlington, VT; and Ellis Mount (EM), Columbia University, New York, NY.

ENGINEERING AND TECHNOLOGY

Building systems reference guide. Edited by Robert H. Perry. New York: McGraw-Hill; 1987. Mixed pagination. $26.50. ISBN 0-07-028802-X.

> This guide reproduces Section 4 and a portion of Section 7 of Perry's *Engineering manual*, 3d ed. (1976). Most of the data are from sources dated prior to 1976. For students and engineers who need only this rather narrow slice of key information on building design, operation, and maintenance. (RGK)

Commercial electrical wiring and design. By John T. Earl. Englewood Cliffs, NJ: Prentice-Hall; 1987. 200p. $29.95. ISBN 0-13-152687-1.

> This work is aimed directly at commercial electrical wiring. It dwells only very briefly on theories and then jumps immediately into the on-the-job applications. Coverage of commercial illumination, however, is treated in greater depth. Excellent and considerable illustrative matter (only drawings). No literature cited. Index adequate. For personal purchase by architects, engineers, designers, building and electrical contractors, and technicians; and larger public libraries. Author affiliation not given. (RGK)

© 1988 by The Haworth Press, Inc. All rights reserved.

Complete guide to stereo television (MTS/MCS) troubleshooting and repair. By Jon D. Lenk. Englewood Cliffs, NJ: Prentice-Hall; 1988. 174p. $29.33. ISBN 0-13-160839-8.

Provides a simplified, practical system of troubleshooting and repair for a variety of stereo television sets and stereo adapters. Assumes familiarity with the basics of television service. Adequate service literature must be available as this book provides only a cross section of stereo-TV circuits. Thus there is no attempt to duplicate full schematics for all circuits. Five of the chapters group similar circuits and in each case there are given circuit-by-circuit troubleshooting actions based on trouble symptoms. For public libraries and personal purchase. (RGK)

Corporate author authority list. 2d ed. Edited by Asta V. Kane. Detroit, MI: 1987. 2 vols. $180.00. ISBN 0-8103-2106-8.

The need for consistency in establishing corporate entries in the cataloging and indexing of technical reports makes this set of great value as it provides more than 40,000 entries. The entries represent those used in the cataloging of all technical reports by the National Technical Information Services since 1979, when its bibliographic database was created, through April 1987. Besides a boldface printing of the entry the nine-digit NTIS code is also provided. There are cross references from nonstandard forms of the entries. Should be a valuable tool for those organizing technical report collections. (EM)

Encyclopedia of building technology. Edited by Henry J. Cowan. Englewood Cliffs, NJ: Prentice Hall; 1988. 322p. $60.00. ISBN 0-13-275520-3.

This encyclopedia is intended for architects, engineers, and others concerned with building technology. The volume contains 210 brief articles by 161 contributors. Each article is followed by references to books or papers containing further information for those who wish to pursue the subject more deeply. Entries denoted by Roman capital letters contain cross references to other more specialized articles. The article on "Tall Buildings," for example, contains cross references to 31 other articles. In addition, there is a detailed index at the end of the volume. The encyclopedia contains numerous illustrations and diagrams. (CC)

Handbook of advanced process control systems and instrumentation. Edited by Les A. Kane. Houston: Gulf Publishing; 1987. 355p. $55.00. ISBN 0-87201-721-4.

This is a practical guide for improving process control as it reflects practices used in the real world. It integrates problems, concerns, and actual experiences in implementing better control and relates them to that technology.

The 60 chapters are adaptations of articles published in *Hydrocarbon Processing* magazine (although actual citations are omitted) and reflect progress of this topic during the 1980s. Users' viewpoints, rather than those of manufacturers, are stressed. For engineers, technicians, and management. (RGK)

Handbook of hydraulic engineering. By Armando Lencastre. New York: Halstead Press; 1987. 540p. $175.00. ISBN 0-470-20828-7.

This is a translation from the Portuguese of the 1983 edition of *Hidráulica Geral*. It provides a wealth of information on hydraulic principles to assist designers in that field. The basis is on applications from world-wide engineering projects. A monumental source book and includes, as a feature, fundamental algorithms. Over 200 tables of data and graphs included. For civil, mechanical, and agricultural engineers. Author with New University of Lisbon, Portugal. (RGK)

Handbook of separation process technology. Edited by Ronald W. Rousseau. New York: Wiley-Interscience; 1987. 1010p. $69.95. ISBN 0-471-89558-X.

Separation processes are central to the petroleum, chemical, petrochemical, pulp, pharmaceutical, and mineral industries. The field of separation processes is broad, encompassing subject matter that ranges from phase-equilibrium thermodynamics to hardware design. It is the objective of this handbook, comprised of contributions by 35 experts, to cover in a single volume the operations that constitute most of the industrially important separation processes. Part I of the handbook is a treatment of principles that intersect most separation processes: phase equilibria, mass transfer, and phase segregation. Part II contains descriptions of specific separation processes from distillation to membrane-based separation. A final chapter addresses the question of which separation process should be used in a given situation. This chapter suggests methods for screening separation processes based on matching physical properties of the system constituents with particular operations. It also examines the influence of scale of operation and design reliability on the selection of separation process. (CC)

Handbook of single-phase convective heat transfer. Edited by Sadik Kakac and others. New York: Wiley-Interscience; 1987. Mixed pagination. $95.00. ISBN 0-471-81702-3.

With the enormous growth of the field of heat transfer in the last twenty years, it is no longer possible for one individual to be an expert in even some major subfields of heat transfer. One such subfield of great industrial importance is single-phase convective heat transfer, the subject considered in this handbook by a team of 25 specialists. The handbook is intended to furnish the latest design and research information on the subject to practicing engineers, researchers, academicians, and students. It features a thorough study of natural and forced convection under a wide range of design conditions, as well as of radiation interaction, fouling conditions, and methods of single-phase heat transfer augmentation. Comprehensive design and research information is presented in extensive tables, charts, and empirical correlations for a wide variety of applications. (CC)

Hardness testing. Edited by Howard E. Boyer. Metals Park, OH: ASM International; 1987. 188p. $62.00. ISBN 0-87170-244-4.

This is a practical guide for those working with hardness testing, from the operating technician to the evaluating engineer and metallographer. Most of the presentation involves specific hardness testing methods and applications. Many photographs of equipment and tables of hardness numbers. Also includes directory of equipment manufacturers and suppliers in the United States and Canada. For most libraries dealing with metal hardness. (RGK)

Human factors reference guide for electronics and computer professionals. By Wesley E. Woodson. New York: McGraw-Hill; 1987. 204p. $32.50. ISBN 0-07-071766-4.

The contents of this reference book have been derived from material previously published in *Human factors design handbook* (McGraw-Hill, 1981). A reduced price for this now slim extract (reprint) from $99 to about one-third of that, makes the volume attractive for obvious reasons. However, there has been some updating in the area of "computer human factors," according to the editors, but this is not particularly obvious from the table of contents or the index. There is no bibliography but there is a meager reading list of eight citations, six dated 1968 to 1984 plus two undated. For those without the 1981 volume (still in print) and interested in human engineering. The author is a consultant in the field. (RGK)

Hy-Q handbook of quartz crystal devices. By David Salt. Wokingham, U.K.: Van Nostrand; 1987. 229p. $69.95. ISBN 0-442-31773-5.

Provides an understanding of the electrical-mechanical function of quartz with its limitations, along with fabrication techniques that will cover precision X ray, grinding, polishing, vapor deposition, mounting techniques, encapsulation, and measurement systems. For engineers concerned with the design of systems that involve frequency management. Well-documented and contains some quite interesting illustrative matter. (RGK)

Industrial control handbook. Vol. 2: Techniques. By E. Andrew Parr. New York: Industrial Press; 1987. 453p. $34.95. ISBN 0-8311-1178-X.

This work is the second in a series of three on the topic of industrial process control. It concerns a wide range of technologies, such as techniques in power electronics, pneumatics, hydraulics, and computing. Good illustrative matter. There is no literature cited. For both the newly qualified engineer and the practicing one. (RGK)

Inspection and gauging. 6th ed. Edited by Clifford W. Kennedy and others. New York: Industrial Press; 1987. 654p. $24.95. ISBN 0-8311-1149-6.

A reference work that discusses the place of inspection in industry, describes the recent types of automatic and manual gauging and measuring devices employed, and shows the proper new and time-honored techniques of using inspection equipment. Various duties of inspection personnel are included. A guide to variation control for engineers and technicians alike. Excellently illustrated with diagrams and photographs. Strong index. (RGK)

Maintenance engineering handbook. 4th ed. Edited by Lindley R. Higgins. New York: McGraw-Hill; 1987. Mixed pagination. $79.50. ISBN 0-07-028766-X.

This new edition contains 40% completely new and 30% revised material plus providing special emphasis on using the computer to manage the maintenance function more efficiently. Includes topics such as maintenance of instruments, preventive maintenance, and chemical corrosion control and cleaning. Hundreds of illustrations (photographs, drawings, etc.) are provided. For all comprehensive industrial engineering collections. (RGK)

Marks' standard handbook for mechanical engineers. 9th ed. Edited by Eugene A. Avallone and Theodore Baumeister III. New York: McGraw-Hill; 1987. Mixed pagination. $89.00. ISBN 0-07-004127-X.

A landmark handbook which has been available for use by engineers since 1916 and has been continually upgraded and updated. This new edition is no exception and once more provides both practicing engineers and students with an authoritative and comprehensive reference work. It is interesting to note that duality of units, USCS and SI, is retained. Increased attention is given to the widespread utilization of personal computers by engineers, hence much material included in this work reflects such developments. Note too that there is an entirely new section on robots and robotics. For all physical science and engineering collections in industry and academe. (RGK)

Motor application and maintenance handbook. 2d ed. Edited by Robert W. Smeaton. New York: McGraw-Hill; 1987. Mixed pagination. $69.50. ISBN 0-07-058448-6.

This book was written as a ready reference for engineers and technicians to use when motor-application problems are being considered. Machinery operators and plant maintenance personnel will also find useful information on motor installation, preventive maintenance, and repair. The handbook contains contributions by thirty-three eminently qualified engineers. Sections 1, 2 and 3 offer basic information governing the choice of motor for a given application. Other sections cover in detail information on the application of specific sizes and types of motors, their components, their installation, maintenance, or repair. One section deals with motor noise problems. (CC)

Optical fiber materials and properties. Edited by Suzanne R. Nagel and others. Pittsburgh, PA: Materials Research Society; 1987. 245p. $41.00. ISBN 0-931-83753-7.

Report on a 1986 symposium which provided a rather erudite multidisciplinary forum on the material science and engineering of the fiber form transmissions, especially optical fibers and optical transmission. Included are new methods of preparation and characteristics of these materials and systems. For strong research collections on these new investigations in industry. (RGK)

Optical thin films users' handbook. By James D. Rancourt. New York: Macmillan; 1987. 289p. $34.95. ISBN 0-02-94770-X.

This reference work is intended for the user of optical thin film products and especially those products which are commercially available. Concern is with preparation techniques and their characteristics. Thus users will be able to specify appropriate filters, and to be aware of the limitations which may be encountered. Emphasis is on pragmatic information needed for using, specifying, or designing into an optical system and optical interference filter. Well over a third of the literature references cover 1980-1987. For research collections in optical and electro-optical engineering. Author: with Optical Coating Laboratory, Santa Rosa, CA. (RGK)

(The) packing of particles. By D. J. Cumberland and R. J. Crawford. New York: Elsevier; 1987. 150p. $58.50. ISSN 0167-3785. (Handbook of powder technology. v.6.)

This volume continues an important series on a variety of specialized areas of powder technology. Here a wide range of information on the packing of particles is brought together and will be of interest to those engineers and scientists who have concern with the densification of a powder mass. There is relevance to many industries such as pharmaceutical, ceramic, metallurgy, and civil engineering. Almost 400 citations are provided in the reference and bibliography sections. (RGK)

Plastics mold engineering handbook. 4th ed. Edited by J. Harry DuBois and Wayne I. Pribble. New York: Van Nostrand; 1987. 736p. $59.95. ISBN 0-442-21897-4.

This is a revision of the 1978 edition but only in the second half of the work as the basics in the first half remain the same. There is, for example, a new chapter on blow molding, and there is coverage of the special considerations in designing molds in the multiton range of weight. The handbook retains a concern with the particular analysis, decisionmaking, and work required to effect a well-designed mold. Well-illustrated. Needed for all collections dealing with the manipulation of plastics. (RGK)

Pocket guide to the national electric code 1987 edition. By Marvin J. Fischer. Englewood Cliffs, NJ: Prentice-Hall; 1987. 287p. $10.95. ISBN 0-13-684606-8.

This pocket guide covers only certain topics in the code, that is, those needed more frequently than others. Thus it is very handy and convenient for a broad spectrum of users, such as the design profession. The volume is *not* intended to replace the *National Electrical Code* itself. (RGK)

Pressure vessel design manual. By Dennis R. Moss. Houston: Gulf Publishing; 1987. 236 p. $79.00. ISBN 0-87201-719-2.

This illustrated manual combines in one source the working notes, graphs, tables, figures, design data, and equations that engineers typically have scattered among numerous books, periodicals, notebooks, and project manuals. The manual can eliminate hours of research for designers of pressure vessels by providing a step-by-step approach to the problems most frequently encountered in the design of pressure vessels and related equipment. The material can be used directly to solve problems, as a guide, as a logical approach to problems, or as a check to alternative design methods. All procedures have been developed and proven using actual design problems. They can be modified to incorporate changes in codes, standards, contracts, or local requirements. (CC)

Pressure vessel systems: a user's guide to safe operations and maintenance. By Anthony Lawrence Kohan. New York: McGraw-Hill; 1987. 458p. $42.50. ISBN 0-07-032538-0.

> Emphasis is on a total system approach to pressure vessel safety in order to consider the many risks and hazards, such as fire, chemical reactions, and vapor-cloud explosions. Provides practical information on minimizing accidents to pressure vessel systems to those responsible for equipment specification and who maintain and inspect that equipment. There is also detailed coverage of different types of pressure vessels. *Not* included is information on the design of such vessels. For mechanical engineering collections. (RGK)

Radiodetermination satellite services and standards. By Martin A. Rothblatt. Norwood, MA: Artech House; 1987. 187p. $50.00. ISBN 0-89006-239-0.

> Explains the technical and operational characteristics of radiodetermination satellite service. Included are sections on system architecture, design elements, management, and applications. The work is for those involved with advanced communication or electronic navigation technology, whether from policy, engineering, or business perspectives. Provides numerous levels of information so as to satisfy the needs of a broad spectrum of professionals (e.g., spacecraft vendors, systems analysts, and software vendors). The author is with Geostar Corporation, Washington, DC. (RGK)

Rule of thumb cost estimating for building mechanical systems: accurate estimating and budgeting using unit assembly costs. By James H. Konkel. New York: McGraw-Hill; 1987. 230p. $40.00. ISBN 0-07-044957-0.

> Presents a rather original, proven-in-practice method of calculating preliminary estimates based on "unit assemblies." Applied to all types of mechanical systems, this method uses labor and material take-off costs from past projects to create estimates on new projects. According to the engineer-author, accuracy should be in the 90-100% range. For collections on construction estimates. (RGK)

Scroll saw handbook. By Patrick Spielman. New York: Sterling Publishing; 1986. 256p. $12.95. ISBN 0-8069-4770-5(pbk).

> Provided are easy-to-follow instructions as the author takes the reader (beginner) through every secret of every type and brand of scroll saw, plus an incredible array of outstanding jigs and fixtures for every purpose. Includes over 500 photographs and drawings, not only involving how-to-do-it, but scores of completed projects such as ornaments, signs, (especially) trinkets,

and bevel cut objects with inlays, reliefs, and recessing. Thus we have a definitive work for public libraries and personal purchase. (RGK)

Shock and vibration handbook. 3d ed. Edited by Cyril M. Harris. New York: McGraw-Hill; 1988. Mixed pagination. $76.50. ISBN 0-07-026801-0.

The 44 chapters of the third edition of *Shock and vibration handbook* were written by sixty authorities from industry, government laboratories, and universities. Chapters dealing with related topics are grouped together. The first group of chapters provides a theoretical base for shock and vibration. The second group considers instrumentation and measurement. Subsequent chapters deal with vibration standards, analysis and testing, methods of controlling shock and vibration, equipment design, packaging, and the effects of shock and vibration on humans. The handbook is particularly intended to be used as a working reference by engineers and scientists in the mechanical, civil, acoustical, aeronautical, electrical, air-conditioning, transportation, and chemical fields. (CC)

(The) surveying handbook. Edited by Russell C. Brinker and Roy Minnick. New York: Van Nostrand Reinhold; 1987. 1270p. $82.95. ISBN 0-442-21423-5.

A truly extensive easy-to-read handbook and practical presentation. Although basic principles of survey measurement remain the same, technology and sources of information change, thus permitting this work to reflect modern technology. Considerable illustrative matter. Well-documented with many recent citations. For general and civil engineering libraries in academe and industry. (RGK)

Switchgear and control handbook. 2d ed. Edited by Robert W. Smeaton. New York: McGraw-Hill; 1987. Mixed pagination. $75.00. ISBN 0-07-058449-4.

A heavily revised edition of the 1977 work. It includes essential information on the selection and specification of all types of switchgear and control equipment needed in industry and provides authoritative, in-depth explanations of the design, application, safety, and maintenance of such equipment. Throughout, high attention is paid interpretations of a variety of standards and codes. Literature reference citations are for the most part current but some chapters are seriously lacking in recent references, such as the one on substations or, oddly enough, seismic requirements (as might be required for nuclear power plants); and there are even some without any references at all (e.g., metering and instrumentation). Nevertheless, this is a valuable handbook: comprehensive and thoroughly practical. (RGK)

Transportation noise reference book. Edited by P. M. Nelson. Boston: Butterworths; 1987. Mixed pagination. $95.00. ISBN 0-408-01446-6.

Provides a balanced and unbiased presentation of facts and interpretations of the effects of noise on man relating to the three principal transport modes (road, train, and aircraft). Given, for example, is coverage in each case of noise generation, methods of prediction, and noise and vibration control procedures. Included too are chapters on vehicle noise emission legislation. Rather well-illustrated. For library collections requiring an up-to-date and comprehensive review of transportation noise and vibration. The editor is with the Transport Road Research Laboratory in England. (RGK)

Systems & control encyclopedia: theory, technology, applications. Edited by Madan G. Singh. Oxford: Pergamon; 1987. 8 v. $2300. ISBN 0-08-028709-3(set).

This encyclopedia is a comprehensive reference work covering all aspects of systems and control. The systems may be simple or complex, mechanistic or biological, industrial, economic, or social. Information is presented in a series of alphabetically arranged articles which deal with individual topics in a self-contained manner. At the same time, each article is part of the larger, systematic work. A guide to the use of the encyclopedia outlines the main features and organization of the work and is intended to help the reader locate the maximum amount of information on a given topic. The material is divided into twenty-five separate subject areas, each containing articles submitted by specialists. The last volume contains a systematic outline of the encyclopedia, a subject index, an author citation index, a guide to information sources in systems and controls, and a list of acronyms and abbreviations. (CC)

World aerospace: a statistical handbook. By Daniel Todd and Ronald D. Humble. New York: Methuen; 1987. 226p. $85.00. ISBN 0-7099-4325-3.

Provides a world survey of the industry in statistical form. The first part covers production and distribution by sector (e.g., aircraft airframes, aeroengines, missiles/spacecraft) and by country. Included is a summary for each country of the degree of government intervention. The second part covers technological change and gives graphical representations of trends in product and process technologies. Anticipated developments are not ignored. Statistical appendices cover about a third of the volume. First author with University of Manitoba, second with the Government of Manitoba. For all reference collections on aerospace activities. (RGK)

HEALTH SCIENCES

Bibliography of bioethics. Washington, DC: Kennedy Institute of Ethics; 1975- . $25.00/yr. ISSN 0363-0161, ISBN 0-9614448-2-7.

The subject of bioethics includes many different areas of study, among them: biology, law, psychology, history, sociology, philosophy, and religion. This bibliography pulls together bioethics literature from those diverse fields using an indexing language developed specifically for bioethics. That thesaurus is included in each volume of the bibliography. The 2,050 entries are arranged by subject. Each citation is followed by descriptive keywords and, often, an abstract. Although, 71.3% of the citations are for journals articles, monographs, court decisions, newspaper articles, audiovisuals, bills, and laws are also indexed. Author and title indexes are provided. For those libraries who have access to NLM's MEDLARS, the *Bibliography of Bioethics* is available online as BIOETHICSLINE. (DL)

(The) Burgess directory: computer systems and services for medical practices. 2d ed. Santa Rosa, CA: Burgess Communications; 1986. 277p. $39.95. ISBN 0-8087-6513-2.

This directory attempts to provide all the computer related information a health care professional would need. But, given the amount of new software produced each year, the variety of goods and services available, and the rapidity with which computer companies appear, merge, and fail, no book on the computer industry can ever be entirely comprehensive. Other, more specialized, directories may have more complete lists of publications, addresses of associations, hardware dealers, and facts about online databases. On the other hand, much of the information in this directory is not available in any other type of source. The bulk of the directory consists of descriptions of software designed for health care applications. The software product's purpose, hardware requirements, price, number installed, and name and address of the supplier are presented in column format for easy comparison. In a separate section the editors list over 100 computer consultants who specialize in health care practice management. Another section provides names and addresses of software producers who will create customized software for a fee. A resource for libraries serving health professionals in private practice. (DL)

Current opinions of the Council on Ethical and Judicial Affairs of the American Medical Association 1986. Council on Ethical and Judicial Affairs. Chicago: American Medical Association; 1986. 52p. $9.50. ISBN not available.

> The AMA has chosen to begin this small volume with the American Medical Association's "Principles of Medical Ethics," a one-page document which provides a general outline of ethical behavior for physicians. In the pages which follow, the AMA's official opinions on specific issues in health care are set out. Any library serving physicians should have a copy of this book. (DL)

Dictionary of psychiatry. Edited by Henry Walton. London: Blackwell Scientific; 1985. 170p. $24.95. ISBN 0-632-00972-1.

> Thirteen British and American psychiatrists contributed to this paperback dictionary. The approximately 1200 definitions range in length from one to ten sentences. Biographical entries are also included. The brief but clear definitions make this dictionary useful for students and health professionals in other fields, as well as for professional psychiatrists. (DL)

Physician characteristics and distribution in the U.S. 1986 ed. Chicago: American Medical Association; 1988. 295p. $42.00. ISBN 0-89970-227-9.

> This collection of tables examines numbers of foreign medical graduates, women physicians, physicians in medical specialties, and geographic distribution and primary activity of physicians. Primary activities include patient care, teaching, administration, and research. Geographic distribution statistics are broken down by state, county, and metropolitan statistical area. These statistics are based on data from the AMA Physician Masterfile, a database of information on all physicians in the U.S. and on U.S. physicians working overseas. (DL)

Septic systems handbook. By O. Benjamin Kaplan. Chelsea, MI: Lewis Publishers; 1987. 290p. $44.95. ISBN 0-87371-095-9.

> This handbook provides the principles and concepts necessary to understand septic systems so as to derive workable solutions to practical problems. Coverage involves the handling of underground water, the leaching of soils, and the ethics of many of those who work in this field. The presentation is quite concise yet comprehensive and should be a reference tool for all who design, use, and certify septic systems. The author is with San Bernardino County Environmental Health Services, California. (RGK)

LIFE SCIENCES

BioScan: the Biotechnology Corporate Directory Service. Phoenix, AZ: Oryx Press; 1987- . $425.00 per yr. ISSN 0887-6207.

The fast growth of companies in biotechnology has made it difficult to keep abreast of recent developments in the companies involved in this field. The need for a separate directory of companies is met with the appearance of *BioScan*. It provides the usual directory data (company name, name of officers, corporate history, etc.) as well as special information, such as names of investors, business strategies as well as research and development activities. There is also a list of products in the market plus a list of subject headings pertinent to companies with like activity. Each issue contains the main entry section (filed alphabetically by company name) plus a subject index, geographic index and investor index. A subscription includes the base volume plus five supplements issued per year; each supplement is cumulative so earlier ones may be discarded when superseded. A useful tool in a field of great interest. (EM)

Biotechnology regulations: environmental release compendium. Harlee S. Strauss. Washington, DC: OMEC International, Inc.; 1987. vii, 422p in various paginations. $95.00. ISBN 0-931283-11-6.

The emerging field of biotechnology is surrounded by many complex issues. The scientific, moral and ethical issues regarding the primary research and eventual release or applications of the modified organisms are drawing national attention and heated debate. This reference work has compiled regulations put forth by federal, state and local government agencies. Primary documents are taken from the *Federal Register, Code of Federal Regulations*, and publications by the Environmental Protection Agency, United States Department of Agriculture, and the Food and Drug Agency. Also included are both passed and proposed legislation. A general overview provides a summary of the regulations, including trends of the past and future. An interesting inclusion is the section dealing with the obligations of the researcher. The publishers, OMEC International, have given this work a decidedly pro-biotechnology slant. They are also the publishers of the *Biotechnology patent digest* and *Federal biotechnology information resources directory*. The three-ring binder format lends itself to periodic updates, but no mention of an updating service was made anywhere. This type of publication would lend itself well to updating, especially because the most recent quoted *Federal Register* is dated mid-July 1986. Also, the three-ring binder that the set comes in is poorly-made, and will probably not stand up to heavy use. Although the price seems a bit high for a collection of reprints, it would be well-used in academic, legal, and special collections. (KLK)

Bolton's handbook of canine and feline electrocardiography. 2d ed. By Gary R. Bolton and N. Joel Edwards. Philadelphia: W.B. Saunders Company; 1987. 381p. $35 (est.) (pap.). ISBN 0-7216-1847-2.

> Most people are familiar with the application of electrocardiography in medical practice, but probably few realize that it has also been employed in veterinary medicine for more than a decade. As veterinary medicine advances, more veterinarians are able to treat heart disease among their feline and canine patients through the science of electrocardiography. This manual is designed for just that. The first edition, published in 1975 by the late Gary Bolton, provided electrocardiograms (ECGs) for the dog. The enlarged second edition, published shortly after Bolton's death, has added ECGs for the cat. Following a brief description of the history and theoretical groundwork of electrocardiography is a chapter providing extensive guidelines for the interpretation of ECGs. One chapter explains the ECG patterns generated by arrythmia, and another describes completely normal ECGs. The final chapter provides the readers the opportunity to assess what they have learned. A glossary and detailed index complete the volume. The book is spiral bound for easy use. Recommended for veterinary collections. (KLK)

Wildflowers: a quick identification guide to the wildflowers of North America. By Robert H. Mohlenbrock. New York: Macmillan; 1987. 203p. $9.95. ISBN 0-02-063420-X.

> This clever little guidebook is just the right thing for amateur botanists. It is compact, filled with gorgeous color illustrations, and, above all, easy to use. More than 300 common wildflowers are described here. The primary arrangement of the book is by petal color, e.g. white, blue-violet, etc., followed by flower shape. The descriptions of each flower are brief, describing the flower as a whole, then the petals, leaves and stems. Also provided are the growing season, range and habitat. While many field guides provide individual range maps for each entry, this field guide has only one map, with the United States and Canada divided into sixteen regions. These range maps seem inadequate, and creating a few more regions would not be inappropriate. The inclusion of only one range map is a space-saving device, but it is inconvenient to flip back and forth. Recommended for all libraries and personal collections. **(KLK)**

PHYSICAL SCIENCES

Ada components: libraries and tools. Edited by S. Tafvelin. New York: Cambridge University Press; 1987. 292p. $39.50. ISBN 0-521-34363-3.

> Addresses the exploitation issues of some of the major features of Ada, viz. portability, reusability, and testability plus the environmental mechanisms

for controlling configurations. A guide to problems with the use of Ada in software development and tools needed. Invaluable for implementors of large Ada systems. Compilation from a 1987 conference. (RGK)

(An) atlas of functions. By Jerome Spanier and Keith B. Oldham. Washington, DC: Hemisphere Publishing Corporation; 1987. 700p. $145.00. ISBN 0-89116-573-8.

> Mathematics is the language of science. It allows the scientist to translate physical occurrences or theoretical discourse to paper in a form that can be readily understood and manipulated. The controlling forces of nature can be described by the use of mathematical functions ranging from the very simple to the extremely complex, and the graphical representations of these functions are compiled in this reference book. Sixty-four commonly used mathematical functions are characterized here in terms of notation, behavior, definitions, special cases, intrarelationships, expansions, particular and numerical values, approximations, operations of the calculus, generalizations, cognate functions and related functions. The compilations of tabular data that were common in decades past have been replaced, for the most part, by four-color computer graphics that physical scientists and engineers should find helpful. Algorithms for some functions, such as the hyperbolic Bessel function or noninteger powers x^v, for use with programmable calculators are included. This reference work, a hybrid of an advanced mathematics textbook and a mathematics encyclopedia, is highly recommended for mathematics, engineering and physical science collections. It is well-bound and nicely laid-out. (KLK)

(A) basic atlas of radio-wave propagation. By Shigekazu Shibuya. New York: Wiley; 1987. 778p. $69.95. ISBN 0-471-88183-X.

> This is a handbook which explores *artificially* controlled radio waves and is a translation from the Japanese of a 1983 volume. The author reviews the processes of this propagation covering the past 30 years and especially provides an understanding of the phenomenon under cloud cover. Hundreds of charts and graphs (mainly in lieu of difficult equations) are provided and an excellent chart-index melds the work into a highly useful tool in radio-wave engineering. For strong collections in electronics and communication technology. (RGK)

Cadmium in the aquatic environment. Edited by Jerome O. Nriagu and John B. Sprague. New York: Wiley; 1987. 272p. $65.00. ISBN 0-471-85884-6. (Advances in environmental science and technology. v. 19.)

> A comprehensive account of current research on the chemistry and toxicology of cadmium in natural waters. Initial focus is on the sources, behavior,

and fate of this metal in such water and then there is data on the effects of cadmium on freshwater biota. The work concludes with a review of the analytical chemistry of cadmium. There is heavy documentation throughout but the authors do not claim comprehensiveness. For broad collections on environmental science. (RGK)

(The) CICS companion: a reference guide to COBOL command level programming. By Thomas Robert Gildersleeve. Englewood Cliffs, NJ: Prentice Hall; 1988. 238p. $19.67. ISBN 0-13-134461-7.

This quasi-handbook may also be used as a text for those who know COBOL and who are interested in software such as Customer Interface Control System (CICS). Many case studies are provided and an entire program is given in an appendix. Best for personal purchase and larger public libraries. Author with Dean Witter Financial Services Group. (RGK)

Dictionary of the physical sciences: terms, formulas, data. By Cesare Emiliani. New York: Oxford University Press; 1987. 365p. $19.95. ISBN 0-19-503652-2 (pbk).

This work is essentially divided into two sections: a dictionary of some 5600 terms broadly covering physics, chemistry, geology, and cosmology (including abbreviations and acronyms plus some charts); and a section containing about 100 tables ranging from "absolute dating methods" to "water, world reservoirs." Excellent for undergraduate reference collections, public libraries, and personal purchase. Author: with University of Miami. (RGK)

GaAs devices and circuits. By Michael Shur. New York: Plenum Press; 1987. 670p. $75.00. ISBN 0-306-42192-5. (Microdevices: physics and fabrication technologies.)

This is a most erudite reference work on gallium arsenide semiconductors written for those researching the physics and fabrication technologies of microdevices. These relatively newly-emerged devices are heavily involved in ultra-high-speed applications. There are many hundreds of literature references. For comprehensive physics and electronic engineering collections in academe and industry. Author is with the University of Minnesota. (RGK)

(A) glossary of computing terms: an introduction, 5th ed. Edited by the British Computer Society Schools Committee. New York: Cambridge University Press; 1987. 73p. $3.95. ISBN 0-521-33261-3.

> In this compilation there are 507 common (plus some not so common) computing terms explained in simple language. Fifteen sections are used to cover a wide variety of topics. The 800-term index includes 300 related terms which refer to similar definitions (e.g. "check sum" is not defined but the index refers the user to "control total"). This volume provides a rather painless introduction to computer terminology for use wherever computerese is spoken. (RGK)

How to find chemical information: a guide for practicing chemists, educators, and students. 2d ed. By Robert E. Maizell. New York: Wiley-Interscience; 1987. 402p. $55.00. ISBN 0-471-86767-5.

> There have been many changes in the field of chemical literature since the appearance of the first edition of this book in 1979. The second edition contains four new chapters, including a separate chapter on the development of *Chemical Abstracts* and new chapters on government information resources and services, analytical chemistry sources from the perspective of chemical structure, and a summary and evaluation of representative trends in the field of chemical information. Much more space is devoted to online techniques and sources, and improvements have been made in the chapters on patents, physical properties, and safety and environmental data. The goal of the book is to help the reader find and use the chemical information needed in the best possible way. (CC)

(A) handbook of determinative methods in clay mineralogy. Edited by M. J. Wilson. New York: Chapman and Hall; 1987. 308p. $99.00. ISBN 0-412-00901-3.

> This provides coverage of the practical aspects of the main investigative methods in clay research and at the same time also provides a compilation of scientists familiar with the difficulties of investigating clay minerals. Excellent and extensive chapter references. For comprehensive collections on clay mineralogy, especially analytical aspects. (RGK)

Handbook of reinforcements for plastics. Edited by John V. Milewski and Harry S. Katz. New York: Van Nostrand and Reinhold; 1987. 431p. $69.95. ISBN 0-442-26475-5.

> In 1978 there was published *The handbook of fillers and reinforcements for plastics* but now this new volume (1987) has been designed as one dealing only with reinforcements for plastics. There is also another volume on

fillers for plastics (not under review here). Thus this separate work devoted to reinforcements is a first and concerns the production, design, and specification of a molded end product. It is appropriate for design engineers, material scientists, polymer chemists, compounders, and molders. Some illustrative matter. Documentation generally quite strong. (RGK)

Handbook of thermodynamic high temperature process data. By A. L. Suris. New York: Hemisphere Publishing: 1987. 601p. $139.95. ISBN 0-89116-609-2.

This is a translation from the Russian of a 1985 monograph. It concentrates on various chemical and metallurgical processes based on the use of gaseous reducing agents (primarily hydrogen), and on chlorine conversion processes. Included is the analysis of methods of compiling and solving a variety of thermodynamic equations and a presentation (hundreds of tables) of calculated data for various high temperature processes. For serious physical science collections on high temperature chemistry. (RGK)

Maintaining and troubleshooting electrical equipment. By Roy Parks and Terry Wireman. New York: Industrial Press; 1987. 179p. $19.95. ISBN 0-8311-1164-X.

A handy reference guide designed for use in industrial training essentially for apprentices. Advanced mathematics is avoided; only very basic algebra is required. Personal purchase would not be out of line but essential for libraries in vocational and trade schools. Authors' affiliation not given. (RGK)

Methods for assessing the effects of mixtures of chemicals. Edited by Velimir B. Vouk and others. New York: Wiley; 1987. 894p. $179.95. ISBN 0-471-91123-2. (SGOMSEC; 3) (SCOPE; 30)

This book sets out to identify the limitations, practicalities, and utility of dealing with chemicals in mixtures as related to exposure of people and nonhuman biota to them. This voluminous (and rather expensive) work provides suggestions for further study and research in connection with the identifications needed. A mandatory acquisition dealing with environmental monitoring and toxicity testing for chemical industry, government, and academe. (RGK)

Multiphase science and technology. Vol. 3. Edited by G. F. Hewitt and others. New York: Hemisphere; 1987. 501p. $89.95. ISBN 0-89116-561-4.

This volume continues a series intended to provide overviews in multiphase systems. Nonspecialist readers will gain a vital update on any number of subjects. The first part deals with closure laws for the framework of the two-fluid model. A second part contains some twenty data sets against which models can be tested. A final part presents benchmark problems (numerical methods). Though highly erudite, the essays and problems (not exercises) provide a well-rounded handbook for serious researchers on vapor-liquid equilibrium, ebullition, and cooling. (RGK)

Numerical and physical aspects of aerodynamic flows III. Edited by Tuncer Cebeci. New York: Springer-Verlag; 1986. 484p. $49.00. ISBN 0-387-96281-6.

Even though this is a partial report of a conference, it is a high-level reference work on aerodynamic flows and provides, as its emphasis, the calculation of flows relevant to aircraft, ships, and missiles. Further emphasis is on three-dimensional flows. The interactive boundary-layer procedures described here display great potential for the calculation of subatomic and transonic flows with large regions of flow separation. There is a bibliography of 640 references, the great majority of very recent vintage. For physical science reference collections. (RGK)

Organic reaction mechanisms—1985. Edited by A. C. Knipe and W. E. Watts. New York: Wiley; 1987. 621p. $184.95. ISBN 0-471-91127-5.

As an annual survey (21st in the series) covering the literature, in this instance, dated December 1984 through 1985, well over 4200 references are cited. However, there are some reasonable exclusions or restrictions because of other publications which review specialist areas (e.g., photochemical reactions, electrochemistry, surface chemistry, and heterogeneous catalysis). For most serious chemistry collections, especially those with a high interest in physical organic chemistry. As usual, well-indexed. (RGK)

Physical methods of chemistry. 2d ed. Edited by Bryant W. Rossiter and John F. Hamilton. New York: Wiley; 1987. Vol. IIIA *Determination of chemical composition and molecular structure—Part A*. 624p. $110.00. ISBN 0-471-85041-1(v. 3A).

This is the first of a two-volume set (IIIA and B) on the subject. The work is rather sophisticated and for professionals who are interested in obtaining information provided by the technique but perhaps not experts in the use of the method. Seven major techniques are provided in great detail, all with heavy and recent documentation. For all serious chemistry collections in academe and industry. (RGK)

Reactions of sulfur with organic compounds. By M. G. Voronkov and others. New York: Consultants Bureau; 1987. 421p. $79.50. ISBN 0-306-10978-6.

> This is an exhaustive reference work (not a translation) dealing with the reactions of elemental sulfur with organic compounds which have accumulated during the past two centuries. An effort has been made to include all the relevant literature published up to the beginning of 1981. 2511 references are cited. Of especial interest are sections on sulfur dyes and vulcanization. The subject index is extensive. For academic and industrial research chemists. (RGK)

Regular variation. By N. H. Bingham and others. New York: Cambridge University Press; 1987. 491p. $75.00. ISBN 0-521-30787-2. (Encyclopedia of mathematics and its applications; 27.)

> A volume which continues a most sophisticated encyclopedia on mathematics, with this portion involving calculus and functions and real variables. An extensive section is devoted to the Karamata Theory and with somewhat less attention to other theorems (but not necessarily less important ones). A good background in graduate level mathematics is requisite. The work (and indeed the whole series) is intended for those with a taste for classical analysis. Extensive references are cited. First author with University of London. (RGK)

Sources and fates of aquatic pollutants. Edited by Ronald A. Hites and S. J. Eisenreich. Washington, DC: American Chemical Society; 1987. 558p. $99.95. ISBN 0-8412-0983-9. (Advances in chemistry series 216.)

> This handbook examines processes such as controlling the transport and fate of inorganic and organic species in the liminic and marine environment. Some of the material contrasts processes occurring in marine and freshwater systems. The theme, explicitly or implicitly, is the relationship between physical mixing and chemical reaction rates. The many case studies serve to integrate information on three processes (e.g., air-water processes) into a system-wide picture of the cycling of inorganic and organic chemicals. Some of the less popular areas of environmental research (e.g., acid rain and PCBs) are also covered. A very handy and thorough approach to water chemistry for academe, government, and industry. (RGK)

Surface crystallographic information service: a handbook of surface structures. Edited by J. M. MacLaren and others. Dordrecht, Holland: Reidel Publishing;

1987. 352p. $79.00. ISBN 90-277-2503-9. (Sold and distributed by Kluwer Academic Publishers, Norwell, MA.)

A strong compilation of the hundreds of determinations of atomic configurations at surfaces which exist are reported in the literature today. The format for each determination is quite compact but complete. A lengthy and thorough introduction to the catalog is provided and then followed by alphabetic indexes of common names and of author's names. The table itself involves 284 datasheets (one per determination page). Finally there are 71 graphic figures representing most structures described in the volume. For all surface chemists, material scientists, and physicists whose work involves crystallography. (RGK)

SCIENCE, GENERAL

International research centers directory 1988-89. 4th ed. Detroit: Gale: 1988. 2 vols. $360.00. ISBN 0-8103-4362-2.

Presents descriptions of more than 6,000 research centers, including entries from approximately 145 countries. Organizations named here are sponsored by governments, universities, independent nonprofit groups, and commercial organizations. This edition contains some 1800 more entries than the third edition. It would appear from the index that around 75% of the entries show a relation to science and technology, with other disciplines such as the social sciences making up the remainder of the contents. A typical entry gives the usual information on location and address plus parent organization (if any). A particularly useful field included in descriptions is that of research activities and publications. There are three indexes: name and keyword index (taken from the title of the organizations), country index and subject index. Staff sizes are shown for each entry, giving a breakdown of professionals versus technicians and other support personnel. (EM)

Milestones in science and technology: the ready reference guide to discoveries, inventions, and facts. Compiled by Ellis Mount and Barbara A. List. Phoenix: Oryx Press; 1987. 141p. $29.95. ISBN 0-89774-260-5.

Consists of 1000 events and inventions representing all areas of science and technology. Each entry includes an additional source of information. Four indexes provide access by name of inventor or scientist, date of the event, nationality of people involved and broad discipline (like physics or civil engineering) to which event/invention belongs. Time period covered by the entries ranges from 25,000 B.C. to 1987. (EM)

Who's who in science in Europe: a biographical guide in science, technology, agriculture and medicine. 5th ed. London: Longman's; 1987. (Dist. by Gale) 3 vols. $695.00. ISBN 0-582-90114-6.

This set provides biographical sketches for approximately 21,000 scientists in Western and Eastern Europe. Turkey is included but difficulties in obtaining reliable information about scientists in the U.S.S.R. caused the elimination of entries from that country. Only those involved in the natural and physical sciences, engineering, agriculture and medicine are included, thus excluding social scientists, political scientists and certain related fields. The main portion of the book consists of the listing of entries alphabetically by surname. There is an index by country, subdivided by disciplines, such as aeronautics, biochemistry, civil engineering and zoology. Typical entries provide such extra features as job experience, professional society memberships, publications and fields of greatest interests. The subject index uses what the entrants consider to be their three fields of greatest interest. (EM)

SCI-TECH ONLINE

Ellen Nagle, Editor

DATABASE NEWS

CHEM-INTELL Announced

DIALOG has added a new database which provides information on the chemical industry. CHEM-INTELL covers chemical plants and chemical trade and production statistics worldwide. Available as File 318, the database produced by Chemical Intelligence Services, a division of Reed Telepublishing Ltd., provides information on plant ownership and plant capacities as well as trade and production figures on over 100 organic chemicals. Data in the file are divided between two unique subfiles. Records in the Plant Reports subfile concern chemical processes; feedstocks; plant ownership, location, and capacity. The Trade and Production Statistics subfile provides production quantities for the latest ten years and export and import figures, including a detailed two-year trade breakdown identifying the countries, quantities, and deduced value of exported or imported chemicals.

Sources for the file are diverse. The Plant Report subfile information comes from direct correspondence with producers, plant contractors, and licensors; company reports; press releases; market and industry surveys; and a comprehensive range of publications. Data in the Trade and Production Statistics subfile are obtained directly from customs authorities, international statistical office publications, trade associations, and selected periodicals and research reports.

Records from each of the two subfiles contain distinctly different types of information. Searchable data in the Plants Report Subfile include details about individual manufacturing plants, while data in the Trade and Production Statistics subfile consist of quantities and values in U.S. dollars for chemicals imported by and exported from a country. CHEM-INTELL contains approximately 20,000 current records. The file is updated monthly, with approximately 1,000 records added or revised per update. The price for using the file is $55 per hour, $2.00 per full Plant Report record printed, and $16.50 per full Trade and Production Statistics record. The file is available through the Classroom Instruction Program.

BRS Offers Current Contents Online

Current Contents Search is online from BRS. The database is equivalent to the five scientific editions of the Current Contents series of publications produced by the Institute for Scientific Information (ISI):

1. Clinical Practice
2. Life Sciences
3. Engineering, Technology and Applied Sciences
4. Agriculture, Biology and Environmental Sciences
5. Physical, Chemical and Earth Sciences.

In printed form, *Current Contents* is a weekly service that reproduces the tables of contents from current issues of leading journals in many fields. *Current Contents Search* consists of a three-month rolling file containing approximately 168,000 records and is updated weekly.

Tables of contents of specific journal issues can be printed online. Subject and author searches can also be performed to find the latest information, unrestricted to particular titles. SDI profiles may be constructed as well.

Whenever possible, the database provides author addresses; the author to whom a researcher should write for reprints is indicated with the notation "Reprint." In addition, copies of articles are available directly from ISI through their Genuine Article service. Articles can be requested online, or may be ordered from ISI by telephone at (215)386-4399. ISI will send original tear sheets or high quality photocopies of articles. Order will be processed within 48 hours of receipt of your request.

DIOGENES Introduced from DIALOG

A major resource for U.S. government drug regulation information has been announced by DIALOG. DIOGENES (File 158) contains news stories and unpublished documents relating to the United States regulation of pharmaceuticals and medical devices. Whether you need to know the federally-mandated performance standards for sunlamps, warnings that should be on drugs containing sulfites, or information on any of a broad range of questions related to drug or medical device regulations, DIOGENES can lead to the answers.

DIOGENES is produced by FOI Services, Inc. and Washington Business Information, Inc. (WBI). FOI is a document-delivery firm specializing in retrieving unpublished government information under the Freedom of Information Act. WBI is a newsletter-publishing firm that produces several health care newsletters dating back to 1981. DIOGENES covers information relating to the U.S. Food and Drug Administration (FDA) regulation of drugs and medical devices, including listings of approved products, experience reports for devices, documentation of the approval process for specific products, and recall and regulatory action documentation.

DIOGENES consists of three main types of information:

1. Unpublished FDA documents acquired under the Freedom of Information Act, not covered in any other database. These documents include advisory committee minutes, drug and device approval information, regulatory letters, establishment inspection reports, industry/FDA correspondence, and many others. Many of the more substantive and timely documents include the full text online, and all documents are available from FOI Services.

2. The full text of newsletters published by WBI. The newsletters include *Washington Drug Letter*, *The GMP Letters*, *Washington Health Costs Letter*, *The Food and Drug Letter*, and *Devices and Diagnostics Letter*.

3. Other full-text FDA documentation, including Federal Register Notice summaries, complete listings of FDA-approved drugs and devices, Enforcement Reports, Medical Device Report incident summaries, press releases, and speeches by FDA officials.

DIOGENES is designed to serve as a resource for those in the health care industry who need regulatory information. These sectors include pharmaceutical and medical device manufacturers, hospitals, research centers (particularly those involved in clinical studies), blood banks, laboratories, and law schools.

The complete text of many DIOGENES documents is available in the online file. Several data fields provide access to drug and medical device information. Each drug listing contains comprehensive data, such as the drug names; New Drug Application number; dosage form, strength, and route; date of approval, discontinuance, and withdrawal of FDA approval to market; and patent number and dates for patent records. The names of companies associated with a drug or a medical device are also searchable.

DIOGENES begins with approximately 150,000 records. Records for unpublished documents date from 1976 forward, and records for newsletters from 1981 forward. The file is updated weekly with approximately 250 records per update. The price for searching DIOGENES is $1.75 per minute ($105 per hour), $1.95 per full record printed online, and $4.00 per full record containing the complete text PRINTed offline. Records without complete text are priced at $0.59 per full record printed online.

Federal Technology Database

Information on federally developed technologies can be accessed through the Federal Applied Technology Database on BRS. Businesses and libraries doing research in new product development will welcome Federal Applied Technology Database. Its purpose is to provide information on federally developed technologies that have applications in the private sector.

FATD is composed of three sections: federal laboratory resources; selected new federal technologies; and U.S. owned inventions which are available for licensing by businesses. Each section may be searched individually.

The database provides contact names and phone numbers in

many of its entries, as well as backup information. All entries contain abstracts.

This unique database is produced by the Center for the Utilization of Federal Technology (CUFT), which is a part of National Technical Information Service (NTIS).

For more information on the database, contact the producer: U.S. Department of Commerce, National Technical Information Service, Center for the Utilization of Federal Technology, Springfield, VA 22161. 701-487-4838.

Major Enhancements Added to DIALOG Medical Connection

Earlier this year DIALOG introduced Medical Connection, a new database service tailored especially for practicing physicians, biomedical researchers, and other health professionals. The service provides fast, easy, and cost-effective access to comprehensive, up-to-date medical information. Both a menu mode for new users and a command mode for more experienced users are available to help you get the needed results.

DIALOG recently announced two major enhancements to Medical Connection which strengthens its ability to serve the information needs of health professionals and researchers. A new Science/Technology Reference Library joins the Medical, Bioscience, and General Reference Libraries. The new grouping of databases adds more general science-related and engineering-related information to the service, just the kind of information needed for all of your background medical research. In addition to the new library, DIALOG also added the capability for searching author names in DIALOG Medical Connection's Menu Mode.

Five new databases comprise the Science/Technology Library: SCISEARCH (1984-); INSPEC (1977-); CA SEARCH (1967-); NTIS (1964-); COMPENDEX (1970-).

The complete DIALOG Medical Connection package is priced at only $145 and includes a self-instructional *User's Guide, A Quick Reference Card*. DIALOGLINK's *Communications Manager*, a password and $100 of free connect time in the first 30 days. The package without DIALOGLINK is priced at $95.

SEARCH SYSTEM NEWS

DIALOG OneSearch

DIALOG has announced OneSearch, a new feature that enables you to search multiple databases with a single command. With OneSearch you can not only compare search results across files, but also modify your search terms, combine search terms, and display results. This important addition to the DIALOG search service allows you to search up to 20 files at the same time, producing combined results and output.

With OneSearch, it is now possible to begin searching in more than one file. Select terms to be processed in each file, and type, display, or print your search results. Searching in multiple databases is easy, allowing you to complete multidisciplinary searches in one step instead of many. DIALOG OneSearch makes searching multiple databases as easy as searching a single database, and is more efficient than searching multiple files individually. Searchers should bear in mind that they are charged for each database being searched. Fields, vocabulary and other characteristics unique to each database must be considered in determining search strategy.

EDUCATION

NLM Student Code Program

The National Library of Medicine has announced a new Student Code Program, designed to make it possible for an increased number of students to access and search most of NLM's databases at reduced rates. Students enrolled in a wide range of educational programs, high school through professional residencies in the United States, are eligible. Two types of student programs are offered:

1. A student who is enrolled in graduate or professional school or in a residency program may apply for an Individual Student Code. This code will be active for two years and the student is responsible for all charges incurred. At the end of two years the code will be converted to regular billing.

2. Institutional Student Codes may be obtained by educational institutions from high school through university level and for hospitals providing residency programs. Institutions may request one or

more codes to be used by one or more students. The name and educational level of each student using a code is requested. Institutional Student Codes are effective for one year but may be renewed by the institution. An institution may provide an Institutional Student Code to an individual for as long as the individual is a student at the institution. Institutions may set a limit on the number of hours their codes may be used.

Student Codes are billed at approximately 50% of the regular prime time and nonprime time NLM MEDLARS online charges. (For MEDLINE student use, this will be approximately $12.00 per hour prime time and $8.00 per hour nonprime time.) Offline prints are billed at the regular rates. Royalty charges for CHEMLINE, TOXLIT, and TOXLIT65 apply. TOXNET databanks, PDQ and MEDLEARN are not searchable with the Institutional Student Codes but may be searched using the Individual Student Codes. NLM is working towards offering access to all MEDLARS systems/databases in the future. All students may use their codes with the GRATEFUL MED software.

Schools currently participating in NLM's Educational Code Program will be transferred to the Student Code Program. Individual students who already have their own access codes should contact NLM to obtain the forms necessary to switch from regular billing to reduced billing for two years. The code concerned must be identified to NLM when the paperwork is returned. Students and institutions interested in applying for this program should request a Student Code Application from: MEDLARS Management Section, National Library of Medicine, 8600 Rockville Pike, Bethesda, MD 20894. Phone: M-F, 8:30 a.m. – 5:00 p.m. ET at (800) 638-8480 (outside Maryland) or (301) 496-6193.

PUBLICATIONS AND SEARCH AIDS

Free Heilbron User's Guide

A new search aid is available free of charge from Chapman and Hall Ltd., producer of Heilbron, the chemical properties database. The *Heilbron User's Guide* describes the database content, the selection of data indexed, and the main Heilbron search options.

To order your copy of the *Heilbron User's Guide*, contact: Jane

Macintyre, Chapman and Hall Ltd., 11 New Fetter Lane, London EC4P 4EE, United Kingdom. Telephone: 01-583-9855, Telex: 263398; DIALMAIL: 12070.

Tree Trimmer

The 1988 edition of *The Tree Trimmer: A Search Tool for Multiple Tree Explosions in Medical Subject Heading* is now available for ordering from Clintworth Publications. The new edition of this annual publication incorporates all of the changes to the National Library of Medicine's 1988 Medical Subject Headings (MeSH).

MEDLINE searchers will find *The Tree Trimmer* to be a timesaver during search strategy construction because *The Tree Trimmer* displays only the unique tree structures for all MeSH terms having more than one explodable tree number. Thus, *The Tree Trimmer* eliminates the need to look up each tree number individually and to cross-compare the contents of each tree structure. *The Tree Trimmer* also identifies the tree number(s) that should be used if comprehensive retrieval is desired.

Searchers will also find *The Tree Trimmer* to be an indispensable resource for use with requestors during the search interview, allowing hierarchy decisions to be made quickly and accurately.

The price for the publications is $35.00 (shipping included) for U.S. and Canadian orders. California residents please add sales tax. Orders from outside the U.S. or Canada will be shipped airmail and will be charged an additional $15.00. A remittance from outside the U.S. should be in the form of an international money order or a check drawn on a U.S. bank. Prepayment must accompany all orders. Please make check payable to: Clintworth Publications, 3336 Waverly Drive, Los Angeles, CA 90027.

SCI-TECH IN REVIEW

Karla J. Pearce, Editor
Giuliana Lavendel, Associate Editor

TIME MANAGEMENT

Berner, Andrew. The importance of time management in the small library. *Special Libraries*. 87(4): 271-276; 1987 Summer.

According to the author, concerns about time management are just beginning to be addressed in the library community. This is a particular problem in libraries where a staff of a few people perform many different tasks. As in a large library, tasks must be performed both efficiently and effectively, despite constant interruptions and the need, on occasion, to let routine tasks go in favor of finding solutions to larger problems. He notes some common misconceptions about time management and lists some of the topics that should be covered in a course on it. Although one might disagree with the author that concerns about time management are new to libraries, most of us need to find ways to work better, faster and more effectively. (KJP)

LIBRARIES OF THE FUTURE

Govan, James F. Fluidity and intangibility: the stunning impact of an expanded information base. *Journal of Library Administration*. 8(2): 15-25; 1987 Summer.

Human information capabilities are expanded greatly by new technology, to the point of changing human intellectual processes. As information access and use changed with Gutenberg, so will our "conceptual universe," bounded by the static information on a printed page. Use of techniques from cognitive psychology to determine the best type of online catalog, expert systems for reference work and information networks are all ideas that were created or enhanced by the new technology. Because of these new capabilities, librarians will be called upon to help users to take full advantage of increased access to and electronic transmittal of information. Librarians must dwell in, and master, a world which combines print and electronics and our "thinking base" must expand to fit that world. (KJP)

A LITTLE HELP FROM YOUR FRIENDS

Marmion, Dan. Taking advantage of users groups. *Small computers in libraries*. 7(8): 10-14; 1987 September.

There are many advantages to joining a microcomputer users group. Initially it provides the opportunity for an exchange of ideas and experiences. The successful ones will grow, creating sub-groups devoted to particular applications (SIGs). User groups also can negotiate with vendors to give group purchase discounts and, naturally, to offer demonstrations of their latest software programs. Those with microcomputers in their libraries can profit by joining one of these groups. The applications you would like to plan for your library may be similar to ones that have been used by your local hackers. There are also groups devoted particularly to microcomputers in libraries, the largest of which is the Apple Library Users Group. Formed in 1983 by the corporate librarian for Apple, its membership includes more than nine thousand members. Or, if you can't find one locally that interests you, why not start one? (KJP)

TAMING THE VDT

Martell, Charles. Automation, quality of work life and middle managers. *Library Administration and Management*. 1(4): 134-138; 1987 September.

Middle managers must constantly balance the "conflicting expectations" of senior management and staff. Issues relating to automation — its impact in relation to other library technologies, its influence on "quality of work life" and the often ambiguous nature of the middle manager's role in automation decisions — are often analogous to the other problems found in a middle manager's day. Her/his authority and the staff's perceived control over their job responsibilities will often be reduced by automation. One way to increase the level of commitment to the new system is to investigate job redesign when automated processes are introduced. A recent study found that even employees who were pleased with the opportunities for career growth offered by the acquisition of computer skills, reported suffering from the many physical stress symptoms familiar to long term VDT users. The author quotes several interesting studies on the subjects and makes useful suggestions for solutions of automation-induced problems. (KJP)

CHOOSING AN AUTOMATED SYSTEM VENDOR

Monahan, Michael. Vendor viability. *Library HiTech*. 5(3) consecutive issue 19: 25-28; 1983 Fall.

When choosing a vendor of automated services, librarians would do well to consider its commercial staying power as well as whether the system can perform Boolean operations or offers authority control. Although the overall picture is heathy, there are serious problems faced by companies that sell automated systems to libraries. In 1986, for instance, OCLC was the only vendor whose new installations matched its historic market share. The market is shrinking. These companies' sales are small by any standard — those of CLSI, the largest, are less than one-sixth the size of the smallest company on Datamation's list of the top 100 computer industry firms. Most of them rely almost exclusively on library automation activities for their revenues, a market which has so far not provided high profits. The companies also lack maturity; most of them, in fact, have existed for less time than the life expectancy of their first products (five years). The author suggests, therefore, that potential customers factor the possible costs for vendor failure when projecting figures for automation. It's a tough world out there. (KJP)

BIND EVERYTHING?

Presley, Roger L.; Landram, Christina. The life expectancy of paperback books in academic libraries. *Technical Services Quarterly*. 4(3): 21-31; 1987 Spring.

Binding of new paperbacks is a costly operation. In an effort to cut costs, the Pullen Library of Georgia State University revoked its policy of automatically binding every paperback book that was added to the collection. Would it be better to put the book on the shelf, then bind it later if needed? To check this assumption, a randomly chosen sample (208) of new paperback acquisitions was monitored bi-monthly. After a year, 15 could not be found, one had already been placed in storage, leaving 192 for examination. 45% had circulated; only 4% needed rebinding. None of them had broken spines, missing covers or loose pages. It was found that books that had not circulated were as damaged, presumably by poor shelving, as those experiencing frequent circulation. They felt that the study supported the decision to discontinue blanket binding of all paperback books. (KJP)

HOW MANY TERMINALS?

Taylor, Jr., Raymond G. Determining the minimum number of on-line terminals needed to meet various library service policies. *Information Technology and Libraries*. 6(3): 197-205; 1987 September.

When making the transition from a card to an online catalog, librarians must make many decisions on purchase of equipment. Focusing on one of them, the author notes the variables to be studied when determining how many terminals to buy for online catalog access. The independent variables he suggests for consideration are the rate at which patrons arrive at the catalog, the average length of time a patron spends at the computer (service rate) and the service policy of the library. Using the queuing model, he tabulates the number of terminals needed to conform to a given service policy. How long does the library feel it is acceptable to ask patrons to wait to use the computer terminal? The first four tables posit an expected average wait time from one minute to less than five, comparing mean arrival rate to the mean service rate. The other twelve tables predict the probability of waiting more than one to five minutes to use a terminal. If you would like to apply this technique to variables with numbers that are greater or smaller than these, the author will make his table generator available. (KJP)

For Product Safety Concerns and Information please contact our EU
representative GPSR@taylorandfrancis.com
Taylor & Francis Verlag GmbH, Kaufingerstraße 24, 80331 München, Germany

www.ingramcontent.com/pod-product-compliance
Lightning Source LLC
Chambersburg PA
CBHW052133300426
44116CB00010B/1880